My Foreign Affairs

From Hubert Humphrey's Vietnam to America's Role on the World Stage

John E. Rielly

T0376339

LITTLE CREEK PRESS
MINERAL POINT, WISCONSIN

Copyright © 2025 John E. Rielly

All rights reserved. No part of this publication may be reproduced, distributed, or transmitted in any form or by any means, including photocopying, recording, digital scanning, or other electronic or mechanical methods, without the prior written permission of the publisher, except in the case of brief quotations embodied in critical reviews and certain other noncommercial uses permitted by copyright law. For permission requests or other information, please send correspondence to the following address:

Little Creek Press
5341 Sunny Ridge Road
Mineral Point, WI 53565

ORDERING INFORMATION
Quantity sales. Special discounts are available on quantity purchases by corporations, associations, and others. For details, contact info@littlecreekpress.com

Orders by US trade bookstores and wholesalers.
Please contact Little Creek Press or Ingram for details.

Printed in the United States of America

Cataloging-in-Publication Data
Names: John E. Rielly, author
Title: My Foreign Affairs: From Hubert Humphrey's Vietnam to America's Role on the World Stage
Description: Mineral Point, WI Little Creek Press, 2025
Identifiers: LCCN: 2025902812 | ISBN: 978-1-955656-94-8
Classification: Biography & Autobiography / Political
Biography & Autobiography / Historical
History / United States / General

Book design by Little Creek Press

To Irene

CONTENTS

Introduction 1

Prologue 5

Chapter 1 **Northern Exposure** 9

Chapter 2 **Harvard, a Fulbright, and Stepping in for McGeorge Bundy** 14

Chapter 3 **On JFK's Mission** 26

Chapter 4 **A Senate Sparkplug** 30

Chapter 5 **Vietnam Rising** 48

Chapter 6 **Exiled** 57

Chapter 7 **In Asia for LBJ** 72

Chapter 8 **Cheerleader for the War** 88

Chapter 9 **Campaigning Under LBJ's Thumb** 109

Chapter 10 **Too Little, Too Late** 120

Chapter 11 **On the Road for Ford** 126

Chapter 12 **Bringing the World to Chicago** 134

Chapter 13 **Upheaval at Home** 158

Chapter 14 **Looking Back—and Ahead** 165

Author's Note 182

Acknowledgments 187

Index 188

INTRODUCTION

By Roger Cohen
Paris Bureau Chief, *The New York Times*

At a time of dangerous turbulence in American politics and the passing of the postwar global order, John E. Rielly, a pillar of enlightened postwar American diplomacy, has written an important defense of what he calls "the liberal internationalist approach to foreign policy." Far from the zero-sum game of naked transactionalism that stands behind the "America First" view of the world, this policy placed its trust in cooperation among nations, the belief that democracy would deliver the greater good, and a rules-based international order as the most effective bulwark against war.

Allied where necessary to "a hard-nosed willingness to deal, sometimes aggressively, with bad actors on the world stage," liberal internationalism put an end to Europe's repetitive 20th-century suicides, birthed the European Union and NATO, overcame the Soviet imperium and delivered democracy to wide swathes of Latin America and Asia. It had a good run. Only in the 21st century did China rise, democracy lose its sheen and America lose its way. Rielly, driven by values of decency, fairness and equity instilled in him when a young boy on the vast North Dakota plains, stood staunchly behind the postwar liberal order.

As a foreign policy aide to Senator and Vice President Hubert Humphrey, as a close observer of the machinations of power in Washington, and, for three decades, as the executive director and president of the Chicago Council on Global Affairs, Rielly cultivated an extensive web of prominent contacts, among them former Chancellor Helmut Kohl of Germany. They were united in their belief in open democratic societies, not as panaceas, but as better than any alternative. Kohl praised the Council for "its tremendous importance in building bridges from America and from Chicago to the rest of the world."

Born into a large Irish Catholic family of modest means—his father trucked cattle to market from the northeast of the state—Rielly deployed a fierce work ethic and shrewd discernment to secure a college education and, in 1954, admission to Harvard on a PhD program in government. A Fulbright scholarship brought international experience, and by 1961 Rielly found himself teaching a seminar on American foreign policy. It was the beginning of a lifelong passion for foreign affairs pursued with sobriety and a peculiarly American belief in the possibility of extending dignity to more of humankind.

The halls of academe could scarcely satisfy this sense of mission. With John F. Kennedy's election, Rielly found a job in the State Department working on the new president's Latin American initiative, the Alliance for Progress, described by the State Department as "in essence a Marshall Plan for Latin America." Its aim, in Humphrey's words, was to eradicate the inequality symbolized by "glittering capitals and festering slums."

The means were simple: offer economic opportunity and enfranchisement to people across Central and South America through massive investment and thereby dull the appeal of Castro's Cuba and of northward migration to the United States. More than six decades on, after a presidential election poisoned by "the border" and immigration politics, the idea looks very prescient. But it died a premature death.

Kennedy's assassination effectively ended the program. With the arrival in power of Lyndon Johnson, conservatives who had the president's ear argued against "spending American dollars on other countries" and had no wish to upend hierarchical Latin American power structures. This was a source of great frustration to Rielly, a believer in America's capacity to bring constructive change, not overnight and not through war, but through patient and disciplined deployment of resources in pursuit of clear objectives.

The Vietnam War was, in Rielly's view, a tragic and avoidable mistake, the great blemish on postwar American foreign policy. As he writes, "the domino theory was flawed. It defied history. North Vietnam had been ruled by a communist government for more than a decade, and other countries had not followed. Whether a particular country turned communist had much more to do with the internal situation than with what was happening in neighboring countries."

He persistently argued that "Americanizing the conflict in Vietnam—sending in U.S. troops to supplant the feckless South Vietnamese army" would be counterproductive because the "populace is unlikely to support Western soldiers fighting Vietnamese nationals, regardless of the ideology at play."

Rielly watched up close as Vice President Humphrey was marginalized by the irascible Johnson. Desperate to find favor again and nursing his own presidential ambitions, Humphrey allowed himself to be cowed into supporting a war in Southeast Asia that he never really believed in, even embracing the baseless bromide that held that "if we don't stop them now, they'll be in Honolulu, then San Francisco."

Witnessing the undoing of Humphrey by Johnson, the escalating disaster of the Vietnam War, and Humphrey's subsequent defeat to Nixon in the 1968 presidential election marked Rielly deeply. He has never been a man to bend with the wind. He took away a reinforced view of the centrality of moral principle. Humphrey had collapsed. Diplomatic flexibility was important, but when flexibility became weakness, the result could be dire.

This book spans the decades from the high water mark of U.S. hegemony in the 1960s to the à la carte world of competing powers today. Rielly suggests, despite his opposition to the Vietnam War, that he was too slow to recognize the limits of American power and perceive the deluded hubris behind attempts "through a combination of wealth, technology and military force to successfully transform remote cultures into democratic societies whose values would eventually parallel our own."

The book ends on a note of somber realism. The United States should "prepare itself and its allies to see Taiwan reunited with mainland China, even if that's the result of a military takeover in Taiwan. Would such an outcome represent a serious setback for the United States? Absolutely! Such is the inevitable outcome when a rising imperial power reduces the sway of a declining European power."

George Kennan, advocating containment of the Soviet Union, argued that the United States must "create among the people of the world generally the impression of a country which knows what it wants, which is coping successfully with the problems of its internal life and with the responsibility of World Power, and which has a spiritual vitality capable of holding its own among the major ideological currents of the time."

Today, however, that is far from the case. Rielly writes, "the extreme polarization of American society, the erosion of influence of essential social institutions, the failure to protect citizens from repeated murders by deranged individuals, the gaps between the wealthy and the average citizen—all these factors and more indicate that America cannot longer credibly assert that it remains a model to be emulated."

For an American patriot like Rielly, these words on the fate of Taiwan and on the disarray of his own country cannot have been easy to write. But his distinguished foreign policy career, for all its liberal idealism, was always anchored in rigorous analysis of the facts as the basis for action.

This is a treacherous moment for an American republic led once again by a leader whose commitment to democracy is tenuous at best and who exercises power and magnetism through the stirring of division. Still, to bet against American renewal and resurgence is always dangerous, and Rielly's fine memoir is a timely reminder of the extraordinary and diverse human resources on which this young nation can still draw.

PROLOGUE

In the spring of 1964, Senator Hubert Humphrey and I had a mission. Both of us had been closely involved with one of President John F. Kennedy's favorite programs—the Alliance for Progress. Though largely forgotten today, the Alliance was an initiative that promised a new approach to foreign policy in Latin America, one that moved past Cold War confrontation and militarism and instead highlighted what were considered core American values: democracy, fairness, equality.

For years, the United States had supported the existing power structures in countries in our hemisphere, and that usually meant backing regimes that were dominated by the military or the oligarchy, often a combination of the two. Leadership of that sort typically left social conditions raw for all but the power elites. Spurred in part by the introduction of communism in Cuba, Kennedy wanted to take a new path with his country's southern neighbors. His Alliance for Progress would offer technological help and billions of dollars in aid to encourage economic and political reform.

With a fresh doctorate from Harvard, I had worked on the Alliance in the State Department just as the program was getting underway. Senator Humphrey was Kennedy's right-hand man on the Alliance in Congress, and after a year I joined Humphrey's staff as the senator's chief foreign policy aide. Much of my time was spent on support for the Alliance, which was proving popular in Latin America and—apart from some conservative senators—even in Congress.

But after the assassination of President Kennedy, the new president, Lyndon Johnson, had no interest in changing the status quo power structure in Latin America. Within days of taking office, he effectively scuttled the Alliance for Progress.

Senator Humphrey and I decided to make one last effort to revive the program, or, at least, memorialize its features. We would write an article for *Foreign Affairs* magazine explaining the visionary advantages of the Alliance for Progress approach. Humphrey asked me to write a draft, and I set to work.

At the time, Humphrey was considered a likely contender—perhaps the chief contender—to be Johnson's pick as his running mate in the 1964 election. Meanwhile, the foreign policy issue that would dominate the years ahead—Vietnam—was just starting to draw noisy attention. Kennedy had increased the number of noncombat advisers in Vietnam from 6,000 to around 16,000, but he had resisted sending in fighting troops. Both Humphrey and I suspected that Johnson favored a more aggressive approach, but in that election year, Johnson was staying cagey, promising simply to maintain Kennedy's course.

Nonetheless, I saw that Vietnam was capturing the focus of American policymakers, which I thought was a mistake, not only because that small Southeast Asian country didn't hold significant strategic importance to the United States, but also because the obsession with Vietnam was obscuring truly innovative policies involving our much closer neighbors. I opened my draft with this sentence: "When it comes to American national interest, Vietnam is but a pebble on the beach compared to Brazil."

I showed the draft to Humphrey, and he was pleased with it—except for that first sentence. "I think we should take that out," he told me gently.

I knew what he was thinking. He wanted desperately to be Johnson's pick for vice president, and Humphrey didn't want to attach himself to any comment that could antagonize the volatile new president.

So we deleted the sentence.

We published the article in the July 1964 issue of *Foreign Affairs*, but the promise expressed in the Alliance for Progress virtually disappeared from the U.S. agenda. My deleted observation was utterly overwhelmed by the events that started unfolding within months.

Looking back now, more than half a century later, I continue to think I was correct (even granting that the "pebble on the beach" simile was somewhat overstated). If the United States had recognized its true national interest in the mid-1960s, it would have refocused its reactive and somewhat paranoid foreign policy and its misguided concern about dominoes falling. Above all, it would not have sent combat troops to Vietnam, igniting a war that ushered in enormous damage to Vietnam, to all Southeast Asia, and to the United States itself.

I stayed with Humphrey through his vice presidency, and though my prescriptions on policy toward Vietnam were not followed, I nonetheless consider myself fortunate to have been in Washington at this pivotal moment in American history. I saw how policy was made, how one powerful personality dominated events, how even brilliant players misread and misjudged the situation and made decisions without adequate knowledge. I witnessed the cruelty inflicted on Vice President Humphrey by President Johnson. And I saw how insecurity and ambition—a pernicious combination—can doom a wise and worthy man.

In the years since Humphrey lost his run for the presidency against Richard Nixon in 1968, I have continued to make foreign policy my life's work, first at the Ford Foundation, then for 30 years as the head of the Chicago Council on Foreign Relations, and finally as a professor and writer. I've known and worked with many of the major international players, in the U.S. and abroad. I've listened to them, sometimes argued with them, and frequently arranged for them to present their views to a wider audience. Throughout, I've tried to hold to my own principles, a set of beliefs probably shaped long ago by my family and education back on the plains of North Dakota and Minnesota.

My principles also grew out of a rich period of American history when the country took a vital role in global affairs. By the early 1960s, when I joined the State Department, I was a generation or so behind the renowned Wise Men—the stable of advisers and officials who largely guided American foreign policy in the decades through and after World War II. Their impact remained profound, and several of them continued to serve as formal or informal advisers well into the 1960s. One of them, Averell Harriman, was still in the State Department during my years with Humphrey, and I worked closely with him in several instances. The Wise Men were overwhelmingly

Eastern elites—Groton, Yale, Skull and Bones, Harvard Law School were fixtures on their résumés. By the time I arrived for graduate studies in Harvard's government department in 1954, their thinking and actions had set the agenda for what's known as the liberal internationalist approach to foreign policy. It's one I readily embraced.

That policy, with its emphasis on cooperation among nations and preference for working with democracies, was often exercised together with its counterpart, realism, a hard-nosed willingness to deal, sometimes aggressively, with bad actors on the world's stage. The two policies took turns dominating American diplomacy after World War II, largely vanquishing—at least, until recently—what had been widespread isolationist sentiment.

Throughout my long career, I've had a front-row seat for watching how the U.S. has handled foreign relations, both successes and blunders. For the most part, my views have remained consistent, though I've seen my favored policy of liberal internationalism fail on occasion, and I've worried about the impact of globalization on working-class Americans. As the United States has continued to stumble into armed conflicts in distant nations with alien cultures, I've wondered why American leaders haven't learned more from the debacle of Vietnam.

In these pages, I will walk through my own experiences, from watching the Vietnam War unfold and seeing how it upended the career of Hubert Humphrey, to working with many of the major international figures as the United States solidified its dominance in global affairs. In recent years, I've watched as America's international role has been challenged by forces both external and internal. In writing this book, I've tried to provide context for some of the key events, and when possible, I've tried to draw lessons from the outcomes. Throughout, I'm reminded that the flow of history is not inevitable. Despite the social and economic currents, the interplay of personality with events usually steers the course, often for better, too often for worse.

CHAPTER 1
NORTHERN EXPOSURE

My father's business was buying and selling cattle, a trade he ran in the flat, desolate landscape of North Dakota. Early on, he had learned a hard lesson in the business. In the 1920s, he and several brothers had ridden the boom in livestock prices, sometimes paying as much as $50,000 in 1920s dollars (close to $1 million today) for a prized bull. When the market collapsed, they went bankrupt.

By the time I was growing up, my father had rebuilt the business working alone. He would buy cattle from ranchers around Cavalier, our small town in the far northeastern corner of North Dakota. Then he'd truck them to markets, usually in Grand Forks, 75 or so miles away, and resell them, hopefully for a profit.

Sometimes Dad would buy the cattle in a private transaction, but often the local farmers would hold an auction where dealers bid against each other for the stock. Occasionally, when I was young, he would take me along to these auctions. They were always exciting—the heavy presence of the cattle, the tension of the competition, the rapid-fire calling of the auctioneer. I would sit beside my father, and what impressed me most vividly was the slight sign he made to signify a bid, nothing more than a flick of the finger.

My wonder from those days has stayed with me—the power of an intimate gesture of communication in this specialized world.

Though my education and career have taken me far away from the sparsely settled farmland of North Dakota, my years growing up there in a large, bustling, Catholic family have remained in subtle ways. My grandparents on both sides were Irish and came to this country in the mid-1800s. My father's father became a successful Iowa farmer, and he and his wife had 10 children, five girls and five boys. My mother's family, the Dowds, were South Dakota farmers, with five children, four girls and one boy.

Both families were deep believers in the advantages of education, and most of my aunts and uncles went to college at a time when higher education was rare in rural America, particularly for young women. All five of the girls and one of the boys in my father's family attended college, and several of the girls continued to graduate school. The four boys who suffered the misadventure in the cattle market didn't go beyond high school, but my father was a lifelong autodidact, following world events closely and often reading from the two encyclopedias he kept in the house.

All five of the children in my mother's family went to the University of South Dakota, and my mother went on to graduate school in English at the University of Chicago. She returned to the upper Midwest to teach high school English, and it was there she met my father—I'm not sure how—probably in South Dakota. For whatever reason, they both were slow off the mark. My mother was 29 when she married, and my father was 16 years her senior.

I was their second child, born in 1932 in Rapid City, South Dakota. When I was six or seven, the growing family moved to a large house on several acres in Cavalier, which at the time had fewer than 1,000 residents. Eventually, I had four siblings—my older sister, Mary, and three brothers, Tom, Jim, and Bernard. The small Tongue River meandered through our property, and one of the bright spots of the year came after the spring thaw. The river would bulge, and we would build a crude raft to float downstream, an adventure that terrified our mother, who worried that one of us would fall off and drown.

My father owned several acres of land about a mile out of town, and after a few years we moved there, to a run-down and creaky farmhouse. It had heating and indoor plumbing, but it was a major step down from the house we'd been renting in Cavalier. My mother was not happy, not only because of the condition of the house but also because the isolation wore on her. After all, she'd studied graduate English at the University of Chicago. Now she was tending house for a husband and five kids in a meagerly populated region where there were few, if any, opportunities to teach, which is what she wanted to do. Still, she and my father seemed to get along, and she never indicated her discontent to her boys, though my sister, Mary, later said Mother would confide dissatisfactions to her.

Both my parents took their Roman Catholic religion seriously, but my father was particularly devout. My brother Jim recalls saying the rosary with him on nights when he was at home. Father didn't smoke or drink or raise his voice, but because he was away often on business, the burden of raising the family fell on my mother. Still, on Sunday nights we'd all gather while he played the violin, and my sister Mary accompanied him on the piano. I recall that my father was well respected by the farmers, who seemed to trust him in dealing with the sale of their livestock.

The North Dakota weather could be punishing, but we simply worked around it. My siblings and I would walk into Cavalier to the public school, except on winter days when snow or the bitter north wind would make the trip too cold, and Mother or Father would drive us. Snowball fights were a major activity, and as children we delighted in each storm as the kickoff to a new fight. The summer often brought stifling heat. I had a Shetland pony, which became an important part of my life in that period and provided some entertainment. It helped raise my standing with kids in the area when I let them take rides.

The highlight of the summer for us and for most residents of that rural area was the Pembina County Fair, held in Hamilton, which was about 20 miles from Cavalier. Farmers and kids would bring in livestock for judging, and there were competitions for vegetables, flowers, and cooking. My brothers and I loved watching the harness races. Amusement rides, food stands, and games lined pathways around the fairgrounds. Mary recalls that once I was pitted in a contest with a monkey to see who could eat a banana faster. The monkey won because he didn't peel his banana. Despite losing, I was allowed the consolation of keeping my banana. The humiliation must have been sufficiently powerful that I've completely suppressed the memory.

My father worried about keeping his children busy and out of trouble over the summer, and one year—I must have been about 11—he bought 10,000 tomato plants and put my siblings and me in charge. My mother thought it was folly—a field of tomatoes! But we tended them carefully, and when the tomatoes ripened, we sold them along with some sweet corn from a stand in front of the farm and to stores and restaurants in Cavalier. The business turned a nice profit for us kids.

By then, though, my mother had seriously wearied of living in a ramshackle house far removed from any semblance of city life. The region featured a few small towns like Cavalier, but you could drive for miles across the flatness and see only an occasional clump of trees beside a field and rarely even run across a farmhouse. What's more, both my mother and father wanted their children to be educated in Catholic schools, and there weren't any in Cavalier. So in 1944, the family moved to a white-frame house in Grand Forks, which at the time had a population of about 20,000 and was the home of the University of North Dakota. My father stayed at the rural farmhouse to run his business and drove down to Grand Forks on weekends. I never heard him complain.

Perhaps surprisingly, I don't recall that my siblings and I were upset at the move, though we would be leaving behind our schoolmates and living apart from our father during the week. Compared to Cavalier, Grand Forks stood as a metropolis, with all the excitement that promised. We attended a school run by St. Michael's Church, and I eventually went on to high school at St. James Academy, an institution founded by the Sisters of St. Joseph and run by the diocese. (The school closed in 1969.)

Happily for my mother, she was able to resume teaching, first part-time at the University of North Dakota, which, like other American schools, saw a burst of enrollment from returning veterans bolstered by the G.I. Bill. She later went on to teach high school English at several schools in neighboring Minnesota.

When we moved to Grand Forks, the war was still raging. Rationing was in effect, though because of my father's business, we usually had plenty of gas and meat. I had a paper route and followed the course of the conflict in the news. Like most members of Midwest farming communities, my parents were strong supporters of President Franklin Roosevelt and the New Deal. My father, who followed international affairs closely, only soured on Roosevelt after Yalta, thinking that the president had given away too much to Joseph

Stalin. Soon enough, Republicans would excoriate Democrats on the same grounds, but my father recognized Yalta's consequences early on.

The paper I delivered, the *Grand Forks Herald*, put out a special edition when FDR died, and I remember finding people crying as I dropped off copies. Roosevelt had been elected president four times and brought the country through the Great Depression and a war. Even at that age, I recognized his remarkable impact.

While we lived in Grand Forks during the school year, we kids would often spend part of the summer back at the farm outside Cavalier. We'd help with chores and tend a big garden (though nothing like the earlier tomato venture). Toward the end of summer, we'd help pick potatoes on neighboring farms, earning money by the bushel. It seems somewhat daunting now, but several times my father enlisted my brother Tom and me to drive truckloads of cattle down to the markets in Grand Forks or Fargo. The trucks were large and long, holding a dozen or more cattle. I was probably only 15 or 16, and Tom was two years younger. I doubt I even had a driver's license, but in those days in that region, it wasn't unusual for farm kids to operate trucks or heavy machinery while still quite young. Our deliveries went off without a hitch.

In high school at St. James Academy, I invested much of my free time in debate and oratory and found considerable success. As a junior, I came in second in the state's American Legion oratory contest, in which we had to write an essay and then deliver it in a speech. I regret that I can't today recall the subject. It cheered me, though, that my father would sometimes take days off work so he and my mother could drive me to faraway Minot or Fargo for competitions.

Those verbal skills picked up in debate and oratory would prove invaluable in my work in the years ahead.

CHAPTER 2

HARVARD, A FULBRIGHT, AND STEPPING IN FOR McGEORGE BUNDY

I graduated from high school in the spring of 1950, and that fall I enrolled at St. John's University, situated on a pleasant campus on the edge of several lakes just outside St. Cloud, Minnesota, about 250 miles southeast of Grand Forks. The school had been founded almost a century before by Benedictine monks from Germany whose successors lived in an abbey on the campus.

The college emphasized the liberal arts, and though in those days most of the faculty were brown-robed Benedictine monks, St. John's had a decidedly liberal tilt in both politics and Catholic thought. It was a leader in the liturgical movement to turn services from Latin to vernacular, and it maintained a close association with St. Olaf College, a Lutheran school south of Minneapolis. Later at Harvard, when I'd run into students from Notre Dame—which I'd also considered attending—Georgetown, and Fordham, I saw that my exploration of religion had been far broader at St. John's.

The leadership and faculty at the school held strong international ties—many of the monks had been educated in Europe, and the abbey had connections around the globe. That wider worldview seeped into the teaching and no doubt influenced me as I proceeded with my education and career.

St. John's enrolled about 650 students when I was there, all men. Eugene McCarthy, the U.S. senator and anti-Vietnam War crusader, whom I would later come to know, graduated a couple of decades before me. On the other end of the spectrum, the right-wing icon Jack Webb, the star of *Dragnet* and a strong supporter of the Vietnam War, had also attended the college.

A women's school, the College of St. Benedict, founded in 1913 by sisters in a Benedictine convent, sat just down the road. Toward the end of my freshman year, I was dating a young woman from St. Benedict and went to give her a kiss goodbye for the summer. She promptly informed me she was about to join the convent. I don't think my show of affection drove her there.

St. John's gave me a partial scholarship, though my father paid for a good part of my undergraduate education. At one point, he managed to pay for three of his children to attend private colleges at the same time, even though all of us could have gone to the University of North Dakota at a much lower cost. As his business declined in later years, he couldn't be as generous with my two younger brothers.

I had vague career plans of becoming a lawyer, and I majored in political science, often considered a stepping stone to law school. I did well in my classes and devoted considerable extracurricular time to a student organization, the National Federation of Catholic College Students, which organized meetings and conventions where we discussed the issues of the day.

My roommate at St. John's, Bob Shafer, was active in a larger student group, the National Student Association (NSA), which I learned much later was funded in part by the Central Intelligence Agency as an aspect of what might be called a cultural cold war. It was widely known at the time that the Soviet Union was quietly funding international student organizations, hoping to influence and recruit promising European and Asian students to the communist cause. The American response, through the CIA, was to underwrite competing organizations to promote democratic values and connect with foreign students. The agency's focus on students is not particularly surprising when you consider that many of the early CIA officers were Ivy League graduates, and the agency actively recruited from elite colleges.

In those early days of its existence, the CIA tended to be made up of officers who were politically centrist believers in democracy. Arthur Schlesinger Jr. is said to have remarked once that in the beginning, there were more liberal Democrats in the CIA than in any other branch of government. The idea of countering Soviet efforts to influence the young made sense. Why not foster the cause of freedom? CIA actions in the cultural cold war stand in marked contrast to some of the agency's more intrusive and deeply regrettable episodes of the same general period, such as promoting coups in Guatemala and Iran.

Still, the CIA leadership clearly recognized that government funding of propagandistic student activities had an unsavory appearance; hence, it kept the program undercover. The money was provided through front organizations. When it came to the National Student Association, only select NSA leaders were informed of the connection—in CIA parlance, they were "witting"—and those in the know were sworn to secrecy. The funding remained hidden until a 1967 *Ramparts* magazine exposé, which put an end to the program. Karen M. Paget produced a thorough history of the operation in 2015 in her book *Patriotic Betrayal*.[1]

Bob Shafer was never high enough in the NSA to be drawn into the CIA's network, and, like almost everyone else, he had no notion it was going on. In 1951, before Shafer was involved, the NSA held its national convention at the University of Minnesota in Minneapolis. A dean at St. John's asked me to attend, and I did, with a senior, Dick Culhane. I remember little of the event, except that the future anti-war activist Allard K. Lowenstein was elected NSA president. (Lowenstein later denied he was "witting.")[2]

I became the president of the Minnesota chapter of the National Federation of Catholic College Students. Because the organization wasn't as focused internationally as the NSA, it didn't hold as much interest to the CIA, and it's not mentioned in the *Ramparts* article or in Paget's book. Nonetheless, since the exposé, there have been reports that the Catholic student group received CIA funding too. Given the Catholic Church's fierce anti-communism of that era, that doesn't come as a surprise.

---

1 Paget, Karen M., *Patriotic Betrayal*, Yale University Press (2015).
2 For a discussion of the Lowenstein-CIA controversy, see, for example, MacPherson, Myra, "Al Lowenstein's Tangled Legacy," in *Washington Post*, March 4, 1985.

Like a lot of liberal young people at the time, I opposed communism, but I never had the paranoid abhorrence of it that gripped much of America in those days, as personified by Wisconsin Senator Joseph McCarthy. Indeed, one college summer I worked at a steel mill in Kellogg, Idaho, where the union, the Mine, Mill, and Smelter Workers, was linked to the Communist Party, though as a summer worker I didn't have to join the union. (A beer never tasted as good as it did when I came off my shift there.) To the extent that I worried about foreign affairs, I was far more concerned about Soviet expansion into Europe. That distinction—between terror of communism and concern about Soviet expansion—has frequently been muddied or lost over the years, though I shared the recognition of it with many anti-communists.

Over my career, I became acquainted with a number of former "witting" NSA leaders and with former and current members of the CIA itself. As far as I know, none were involved in militant activities, and to a man—and my acquaintances were all men—none regretted their service to their country through the CIA. Although I would become aware of the many excesses of the agency over the years, my overall experience left me with a positive impression of the CIA and respect for the dedication and skill of the men and women who worked for it. Prior to the establishment in 1975 of the Church Committee—the U.S. Senate committee chaired by Idaho Democrat Frank Church that was assigned to investigate CIA abuses—there was little, if any, careful oversight of the CIA's covert activities. As a result, CIA agents engaged in a number of misdeeds, many of them approved by Allen Dulles, the CIA director throughout the eight years of the Eisenhower administration and the brother of Secretary of State John Foster Dulles. The story floated around that President Dwight D. Eisenhower once said, "I could control John Foster Dulles, but never Allen Dulles." The Church Committee's revelations led to congressional oversight of the CIA and restrictions on its activities.

When we were seniors, Shafer and I raised a bit of hell at St. John's by publishing an underground newspaper, *Squawk*, that devoted considerable space to criticizing school policies. Shafer anticipated the reaction we would ignite, and just before publication of the first and only issue, he prophylactically checked into the infirmary. I was left to take the brunt of the administration's anger. I've always suspected that because of *Squawk*, the dean denied me the role of valedictorian, even though I had the highest grades in my class. In fairness, he and others in the administration and faculty were generous in recommendations for graduate school.

I was accepted at Harvard in 1954, one of 12 students admitted that year to the government PhD program. (Political science was then and is now called "government" at the school because longtime Harvard President Lawrence Lowell didn't think politics could ever become a science.) I learned later that Harvard was happy to accept me in part because one of the few St. John's students to apply to the graduate government department before me, Cleveland Cram, had made an excellent record at the school around a decade before. Cram later became a senior official at the CIA.

My parents, who deeply valued education, were thrilled that I would attend Harvard. I received several generous scholarships, including one known as a Danforth Fellowship, underwritten by the founder of the St. Louis-based Ralston Purina Company. That fellowship, which no longer exists, was designed to attract Christians into higher education and had only recently been reconfigured to include Roman Catholics. I wasn't set on a teaching career. For a time, I thought I might combine getting a PhD with law school—at least, until I saw how hard the law students at Harvard studied and worked. In any case, the Danforth Fellowship supplied not only university fees but comfortable financial support too.

In the fall of 1954, I left Grand Forks and moved into a graduate dorm in Cambridge, taking dinners at Harkness Commons with other students from the graduate and law schools. At least half a dozen of the people I met in those days have remained close friends through the following decades. The chair of the government department was Samuel Beer, an esteemed political scientist and active Democrat who had earned a Bronze Star in Normandy in 1944. My advisor became Robert McCloskey, a quiet and deferential man who was an expert on American constitutional law. I took the usual smattering of first-year courses—political philosophy, American government, international relations, constitutional law. One of the most interesting was a course in American intellectual history taught by Arthur Schlesinger Jr., who, though only in his early thirties, was already a star of the

Harvard faculty. I'd later work with him directly while he was in the Kennedy administration and I was on Senator Humphrey's staff.

That first year, I also took a seminar on contemporary political philosophy with Professor William Y. Elliott, a Southerner who had warned about the fascists before World War II and had turned strongly anti-Soviet and anti-communist after the war. I later learned that he guided a lot of promising students into the State Department and the CIA. His assistant in the course—I thought he was a grad student, but he turned out to be an instructor—was a rumpled, overweight man who looked about 20. He rarely spoke up in class, though he has had much to say since: Henry Kissinger. Upon Elliott's retirement from Harvard in 1963, Kissinger wrote in an appreciation that Elliott had inspired his career and added, "Political theory to him ... was an adventure where good and evil were in constant struggle to give meaning to existence...."

Toward the end of my first year, I decided to focus my PhD thesis on contemporary church-state relations in the United States and Europe. The subject had been a major source of controversy over the last few decades and was growing in importance in the United States, particularly as John Kennedy, a Roman Catholic, emerged as a likely presidential contender. For centuries, the Catholic Church had assumed that church and state should be as one. In Catholic terms, the U.S. separation was suspect, if not outright wrong. But a celebrated American Jesuit theologian, John Courtney Murray, was vigorously challenging that view, arguing that the Vatican model fit a particular period of history but had lost relevance in a world of religiously pluralistic societies such as the United States. He maintained that the American system was every bit as legitimate under Catholic theology. I planned to focus my work on Murray and a French philosopher, Jacques Maritain, who was making similar arguments about the Church in Europe.

That spring, I received a Fulbright Scholarship to study the subject in England. Consequently, in July 1955 I took a year off from Harvard and went to Europe for the first time. Every Harvard PhD student in those days had to qualify in two of three foreign languages: French, German, and Russian. I had studied Latin and Spanish in high school, so I started my overseas year by attending a French language school in Pau, just above the Pyrenees, and later spent three weeks in Paris, opening a lifelong attachment to that city. Later that summer, I began studying German, attending a course at the University of Vienna.

Fortunately, the Fulbright offered a generous stipend in addition to school fees, and in and around my studies, I was able to take my version of the Grand Tour, visiting Germany, Austria, Italy, Spain, Portugal, and Ireland. The trips helped acquaint me with lands far beyond the plains of North Dakota. I enjoyed seeing the wider world, meeting people of different cultures and customs, visiting many places of great historical significance, places I had only known in books.

In England, I started at the University of Durham, which I mistakenly thought had strong resources in church-state relations, but I soon transferred to the London School of Economics and Political Science. As it turned out, LSE was also weak in my thesis subject, and as a result, I decided to take advantage of the school's strong program in international relations. One of the highlights was a seminar on contemporary world affairs taught by Michael Oakeshott, a brilliant and wide-ranging scholar whose political philosophy skewed conservative. The LSE board had brought him in as director to succeed Harold Laski, an outspoken socialist, who had headed the school for several decades. People sometimes said the reason the Indian bureaucracy was heavily socialist was because many of the bureaucrats had studied under Laski.

While studying in England, I met another Fulbright student, Elizabeth Downs, a small, dark-haired, sociable woman who had grown up in the Beverly neighborhood of Chicago. The daughter of a businessman and a housewife, she had attended Beloit College in Wisconsin, then earned a master's degree in political science at Mt. Holyoke in Massachusetts. She was studying international relations at LSE.

We started dating and discovered we had very similar interests. Over the months, our romance bloomed. After the Fulbright year ended in the fall of 1956, she returned to Chicago, then moved to the Boston area so we could be together. She got a job teaching at Regis College, a Catholic school (in those days all women) just west of Boston. She had grown up Protestant but happily agreed to take instruction in the Catholic faith. In Chicago, she learned from a young priest named Andrew Greeley, who would go on to become the noted sociologist and novelist. Father Greeley, who became a close friend of mine, married us in December 1957 at Christ the King Parish in Beverly.

Elizabeth and I moved into an apartment in Cambridge, and she continued to teach until our first child, Mary Ellen, was born in December 1958. Our second, Catherine, arrived a year and a half later.

The Danforth Fellowship included additional funds for spouses and children, and with that money, I was able to take a lighter teaching load than many of my graduate-school colleagues and devote more time to research and writing. I did put in time serving as a nonresident tutor to Harvard undergraduates at Eliot House. One of my students was preparing a thesis on H. L. Mencken, the writer and polemicist, and in preparation I read quite a bit of Mencken. He and I were ideological opposites—he was deeply conservative and a notorious foe of President Roosevelt—but he was a wonderfully funny and gifted writer. I'm sorry Mencken draws little attention today—he was an effective critic of his enemies, and even if you totally disagreed with him, his wit made it fun to joust with his ideas.

Several incidents from my years at Harvard stand out even today. Eliot House had the tradition of bringing in distinguished figures to lecture and mingle with the resident students for several weeks. One of the figures in my time was Dean Acheson, the secretary of state under President Harry Truman. At an Eliot House dinner one night, I sat at a table with Acheson and a handful of students. One young man brought up Portugal, which had been ruled for years by the dictator Antonio Salazar. He led an authoritarian regime, though not on the order of neighboring Spain's Francisco Franco. Among other things, Portugal had remained neutral in World War II, even allowing an Allied air base on the Portuguese Azores Islands. Nonetheless, the student criticized American policy for being too soft on Salazar.

Acheson listened patiently for several minutes, then turned on the student with a series of demanding and increasingly fierce questions, pushing the student to concede point after point until finally the devastated young man, by then slumped in his chair, was forced to concede that his argument was completely without merit. I've always been struck by that image: This elegant patrician, a product of Groton, Yale and Harvard Law School, one of the two or three most influential secretaries of state in American history, rising up to—in the phrase made famous by chess genius Bobby Fischer, "break the ego"—of a naïve young student.

When I selected church-state relations as my thesis topic, friends warned that Harvard was not known to be particularly friendly to Catholics. I only encountered anti-Catholic views once, however, and they came from a fellow student. During my first semester, I took a course on contemporary issues in constitutional law from Arthur E. Sutherland, a Harvard law professor. Abortion wasn't yet a prominent issue, but the question of federal aid to religious schools, including Catholic schools, was being hotly debated around the country, and church-state relations came up for discussion in class.

A Nieman fellow, Anthony Lewis, jumped in and made a passionate attack on the Catholic Church, arguing that it was a threat to democracy. Given his fiery language, he wasn't just testing an argument—he clearly seemed to have a strong anti-Catholic bias. I attempted a futile response. Lewis went on to serve for decades as the Supreme Court reporter for *The New York Times.*

Both the government department chair, Sam Beer, and my advisor, Robert McCloskey, had acknowledged that the department had little expertise in matters of church-state relations, and with their encouragement, I drew heavily on several outside scholars, one from Notre Dame and one from Oxford. In 1960, I also conducted a long in-person interview with John Courtney Murray at Woodstock Seminary in Maryland, where he was in residence.

Murray was helpful and encouraging, but I was far from the only person to interview him that year—by then, John Kennedy's campaign for president was heating up, and journalists eagerly sought Father Murray's opinions. A dominant issue in both the primary and general elections was whether a Catholic could serve as president and still faithfully fulfill the obligations of the U.S. Constitution. Murray, of course, thought a Catholic could.

Because the topic of my thesis was timely, someone in the government department suggested that I offer to advise the Kennedy campaign on church-state relations. I went to see Steve Smith, Senator Kennedy's brother-in-law, at his Boston office. He kept me waiting for an hour but then listened politely as I described my thesis and asked if the campaign would like to tap my expertise. He answered, "It's possible we might, but not likely."

The campaign never called, and I later learned it had retained

John Cogley, the longtime editor of *Commonweal* magazine and a prominent Catholic journalist, as the principal adviser on church-state issues. Cogley is credited with arranging Kennedy's September 1960 appearance before the Greater Houston Ministerial Association, a gathering of Protestant clergymen. Kennedy's speech that day largely diffused concerns about his Catholicism in his race against Richard Nixon.

My thesis concluded that Father Murray had successfully shown that the American constitutional system was fully consistent with traditional Catholic doctrine. Though I never mentioned Kennedy in the work—I was dealing with doctrinal issues, not politics—his election confirmed that the American people could accept a Catholic politician into the White House.

Five days after Kennedy's election, I successfully defended my thesis, and my PhD was awarded a few months later (I actually received it at commencement exercises in May 1961). Meantime, the department appointed me to teach a basic course on American government for the semester beginning January 1961. I set to work preparing for that course.

But a few days before Christmas, Robert McCloskey, who had succeeded Sam Beer as chairman of the government department, asked me to stop into his office. "John," he asked when I arrived, "how would you like to teach a seminar on American foreign policy?"

I said I thought I was supposed to teach a Government 1 section.

McCloskey said he'd just learned that the professor who was supposed to teach the seminar, McGeorge Bundy, dean of the faculty of arts and sciences and a senior member of the government department, was leaving to join the Kennedy administration as national security advisor.

I protested that I had no qualifications to teach foreign policy, let alone lead a seminar on the subject that students expected would be taught by McGeorge Bundy, whose lectures on international relations sometimes drew standing-room crowds from across the campus.

"John," McCloskey responded, "you have the ultimate qualification: You are the most available warm body in the department."

So I took on the job—an assignment that tilted the direction of my career from political science to international relations.

The seminar was part of a unique Harvard program of around half a dozen seminars set up a few years earlier by Bundy. They were offered to advanced first-year students (who qualified as sophomores), and they were taught by the stars of the Harvard faculty—at least, they were until I stepped in. You can imagine the shock of those 12 brave young Harvard and Radcliffe students who had expected to learn from Bundy, a famously brilliant man who had ascended to dean of faculty at 34, and instead faced the greenest face in the government department.

The seminar's subject was the relationship between domestic politics and American foreign policy—an enduring topic in international relations. I had some background, but I scrambled to prepare. In the seminar, I started with the interwar period, after the U.S. Senate defeated Woodrow Wilson's proposal to join the League of Nations, a rebuke that ushered in a period of dominant isolationism in the country. That lasted until Pearl Harbor, which reversed the populist isolationism and pulled the country into active participation in the world. Postwar, some isolationist sentiment bubbled back up, despite the Soviet Union occupying Eastern Europe and posing a threat to Western Europe. But for the most part, the public supported the country's leadership role in Western Europe— funding the Marshall Plan, helping to found NATO, encouraging the founding of the European Union. The start of the Korean War in 1950 opened an active American role in Asian affairs.

The seminar students apparently forgave my inexperience and seemed to respond positively to the class. Coincidentally, one of them, Marshall Bouton, succeeded me decades later as president of the Chicago Council on Foreign Relations. What's more, the seminar's subject—the interplay of domestic politics and foreign policy—figured prominently in the years ahead.

That summer, I enjoyed a deeper immersion in foreign relations as one of two teaching assistants to Professor Karl Deutsch, a refugee from Prague and an expert on European politics, who was teaching a course on international politics. The second assistant was Leslie Gelb, with whom I would again work closely when he was an aide to New York Senator Jacob Javits and I was on Senator Humphrey's staff. Later, after he had overseen the writing of the Pentagon Papers and served as a *New York Times* correspondent, Gelb served for a decade as president of the New York Council on Foreign Relations while I headed the Chicago Council on Foreign Relations.

That was years away, however. My immediate future would land me in the midst of the new political adventure unfolding in the nation's capital.

CHAPTER 3
ON JFK'S MISSION

I enjoyed the teaching, but the election of Kennedy signaled fresh excitement in Washington, and I was eager to participate. At the time, several Harvard professors were actively recruiting students to join the administration. Arthur Schlesinger knew of my interest, and he suggested I become a special assistant to William McCormick Blair Jr., a rich Chicagoan who had served as chief of staff to Adlai Stevenson for a decade and had just been appointed ambassador to Denmark. But with a new family, I was hardly in a position to move to Copenhagen.

A likelier opportunity opened when Sam Beer asked if I was interested in joining the State Department and working on the new Latin America initiative, the Alliance for Progress. This was a favorite Kennedy program that at first was met with great enthusiasm in the United States and in many circles in Latin America. Referencing one of the country's most successful postwar programs, the State Department has described the Alliance for Progress as "in essence a Marshall Plan for Latin America."

Just as the Marshall Plan was intended to push back against communism in Europe, one prime motivation for the Alliance was to provide an alternative mode of development to the communist system that Fidel Castro had recently imposed in Cuba.

Using the Alliance, Kennedy wanted to shift the prevailing American policy toward America's southern neighbors, which for most of the century had centered on encouraging the status quo and maintaining stability. That had meant getting along with the traditional power centers, usually the rich, the military, and the Catholic Church. More recently, it often entailed putting the chief of police and maybe the intelligence chief on the CIA payroll. Most Latin American countries suffered from gross inequality among the population, and many were dominated by the military. For the most part, democratic institutions had hardly taken hold, though some Church leaders were starting to speak out, particularly in Chile and Brazil.

Kennedy hoped that a program supporting economic and political development could change the balance of power in countries throughout the region. The United States pledged $20 billion to the initiative. In addition, the U.S. would provide technical assistance while encouraging fundamental land and labor reform and lending support to reformist elements. Kennedy hoped to enfranchise far more people and enlarge the middle class. In sum, the Alliance for Progress aimed at altering the distribution of wealth and power in Latin America.

Though the Alliance would reside in the State Department, Kennedy had told Beer that he was looking for some bright young people from outside the Foreign Service to help run the program. I was interested, and I traveled to Washington and interviewed with Bill Dentzer, an Alliance official who had been a president of the National Student Association a decade or so before and had gone on to serve in the CIA. (I didn't learn of his CIA connection for several years, and my Alliance for Progress job had nothing to do with the CIA.) After several other interviews and waiting a few months while my hiring worked its way through the bureaucracy, I was offered and accepted the job to begin in September 1961. Elizabeth was enthusiastic about going to Washington, and that fall we moved with the two girls into a rented apartment in Arlington.

Though the Alliance was a State Department program, because it was a Kennedy favorite, it was essentially run out of the White House.

As a result, I had little or no contact with Kennedy's secretary of state, Dean Rusk. In my new job, I was chief political officer of the Alliance Colombia desk. That meant working with economists and other technical experts in and out of government to manage the allocation of funds. On an international level, I also dealt with organizations such as the World Bank and the International Monetary Fund, which were dominated by the United States and gave direct support to aspects of the American program.

Colombia in those days was making a halting transition from being run by a military junta to embracing progressive democratic rule, and together with Chile, it was a favored country for the Alliance program. In 1962, Guillermo Leon Valencia, the son of a celebrated Colombian poet, was elected president. Though a member of Colombia's Conservative Party, Valencia introduced a number of reforms, including an affordable housing project in Bogotá built with support from the Alliance for Progress and renamed Ciudad Kennedy after Kennedy's assassination. For a few years in the early 1960s, Colombia enjoyed a period of relative peace and prosperity before militant factions on both the left and the right—aggravated by American meddling—and the growing drug trade led to terrorism and hardships for the population.

I enjoyed my work on the Colombia desk—at one point, I attended Valencia's inauguration in Bogotá with the American delegation that included the poet Archibald MacLeish. But the Alliance for Progress was running into trouble at home. It took fire from some conservatives who didn't want to see the power structures in Latin America upended; others simply disliked spending American dollars on other countries. The critics found their chieftain in the U.S. Senate in the person of South Carolina Senator Strom Thurmond. A vigorous opponent of civil rights legislation, Thurmond opposed extending rights to disenfranchised Americans, let alone disenfranchised Latin Americans.

President Kennedy knew that if the Alliance for Progress was going to survive, he needed help in the Senate. He called in Senator Hubert Humphrey, who was not only a member of the Foreign Relations Committee, which originated the legislation authorizing the program, but also a member of the Appropriations Committee, which funded it. Humphrey, who had recently toured South America and admired the Alliance program, readily agreed to be its champion in the Senate.

As it happened, Humphrey's top aide on foreign policy had just announced he was leaving to return to academia. Someone—I don't know who—told the senator about me and my role with the Alliance for Progress in the State Department.

I was at my desk in Foggy Bottom one day in 1962 when Senator Humphrey called out of the blue. "I've got a great job for a bright young man," he said. "Come up and see me."

So I did.

CHAPTER 4
A SENATE SPARKPLUG

I'd never met Senator Hubert Humphrey before interviewing with him, but having gone to college in Minnesota, I was generally familiar with his background. He'd grown up the son of a pharmacist and dropped out of the University of Minnesota during the Depression to help rescue his father's pharmacy. That experience—hardship for his own family and for many others during that time—stayed with him and clearly influenced the tilt of his politics. It may also have contributed to a sense of insecurity that later came to haunt Humphrey. He eventually earned several degrees and became a young, progressive mayor of Minneapolis.

I knew that he had unified Minnesota's Democratic Farmer Labor Party in the early 1940s and that he was a founder of Americans for Democratic Action, for years the principal national liberal political organization. In 1948, the year he was elected to his first term in the U.S. Senate, he drew wide attention for an impassioned speech to the Democratic National Convention in Philadelphia, successfully urging the delegates to add a strong civil rights plank to the party platform. Over the years I worked with Humphrey, I came to see that speech as emblematic of his character—he was the rare politician who held to his principles, even when doing so threatened his personal ambitions. I only saw him deviate from that steadfastness a few times, disastrously on the Vietnam War.

On foreign affairs, which increasingly occupied my interests, his views dovetailed with mine. He had battled communists in Minnesota for control of the Democratic Party, but throughout his career, he favored active efforts to seek compromise with the Soviet Union. In particular, he was an outspoken proponent of arms-control agreements. He was chairman of the Arms Control Subcommittee of the Senate Foreign Relations Committee from 1955 to 1959 and a strong advocate of the Arms Control and Disarmament Agency, which Kennedy established in 1961.

I was 29 when I went to Humphrey's office for the job interview. I found a warm, exuberant man in his early fifties. He was of medium height and trim—only later did he put on the weight that would round him out. As I would come to know, he was interested in people, and he loved to talk. He'd run into someone in the Senate hallway and invite him or her back to his office for a chat, completely disrupting his schedule. The lack of discipline could be frustrating, but I came to appreciate his unbending optimism and his faith in the goodness of people. He was more compassionate than almost any other politician of my acquaintance.

Interviewing for the job, I also sat down with Humphrey's veteran administrative assistant, a wily Texan named Bill Connell, who resented people from Harvard and with whom I would have a contentious relationship. But all went well at first—I was offered and accepted the job as Humphrey's foreign policy assistant, joining a staff of around 35 or 40 people.

I started a week or so after the Cuban missile crisis in October 1962. Curiously, I have little memory now of my thoughts throughout those traumatic days, other than my faith that President Kennedy would guide the country safely through. Humphrey wasn't involved in decision-making during the crisis. The participants were current and former members of the Executive Committee of the National Security Council. (One reason nothing leaked was that there were no members of Congress involved.) Afterward, as a senior member of the Senate Foreign Relations Committee, Humphrey was briefed on the resolution of the conflict, and he supported the president's decisions.

Around half of my portfolio in the new job involved dealing with the Alliance for Progress. I worked with Humphrey on the authorization and appropriation processes in the Senate, and we dealt with the State Department and a wide variety of other officials in the United States and around the world. Because Humphrey came to be seen as Kennedy's legislative chief on the Alliance, Latin American officials visiting Washington would want to see the senator.

Though the initiative enjoyed considerable support in Congress, even from Republicans, Strom Thurmond and his ilk rarely missed an opportunity to attack the Alliance or other important Latin American projects. Humphrey invariably responded, often with a speech I'd written. Sometimes, the Thurmond attacks grew painfully personal. For example, a bright young museum curator from Argentina, Rafael Squirru, was appointed to run the cultural department of the Organization of American States, the league of countries formed after World War II to encourage cooperation within the hemisphere. The OAS is headquartered in Washington, and one of Squirru's first projects was to mount an art exhibit at the OAS museum. Squirru knew the direction art was going, and his exhibit was modern and even revolutionary. One of Senator Thurmond's conservative aides visited the show, decided he was appalled, and persuaded the senator to deliver a scathing speech to Congress denouncing this subversive curator.

Squirru was terrified—attacked by an influential American senator. He was sure his boss, the secretary general of the OAS, a conservative Uruguayan named Jose Mora, would have his head. I'd recently met Squirru, and he called me up. I told him not to worry, I'd write a speech for Humphrey. And that's what happened—Humphrey delivered to Congress a vigorous defense of the curator and his exhibit, and Humphrey sent a copy to Mora. The crisis passed, and Squirru went on to a long career as one of the most influential art critics in South America. He remained an appreciative friend.

Around this time, I began to develop a wide network of contacts in Germany, which overlapped in some respects with my work on the Alliance and led to lifelong friendships. At a meeting in Venezuela of the InterAmerican Development Bank in 1963, which I attended with Senator Humphrey, I came to know leaders of two influential German foundations. The Konrad Adenauer Foundation was the political foundation of the German Christian Democratic Party, and the Friedrich Ebert Foundation was the German Social Democratic counterpart. Both parties were broad-based and center-oriented, though the Christian Democrats were slightly more conservative than the Social Democrats. In any case, the foundations attached to both parties enthusiastically welcomed the Alliance for Progress and its goal of overturning the political and economic status quo in Latin America.

To support the Alliance, the Kennedy administration hoped to enlist European investments in selected Latin American countries. One important initiative in that regard was launched by Senator Jacob Javits, the senior senator from New York, a liberal Republican close to the New York business and financial community. He was also a good Humphrey friend.

Javits persuaded the Ford Foundation to fund the Atlantic Community Development Group for Latin America, an organization designed to encourage European investment. To ensure bipartisan support, Javits asked Humphrey to serve with him as co-chairman. The Germans were active participants. Over the course of several years, I attended a number of Atlantic Community meetings, and through those meetings I met many German political and government leaders, including Willy Brandt, then mayor of Berlin. Humphrey would become Brandt's closest American friend, and Brandt and I enjoyed a long friendship. Separately, the Adenauer and Ebert Foundations arranged several trips for me to Germany, where I also met a number of German leaders.

Senator Javits reinforced for me a lesson I was starting to learn about some politicians. Once, I accompanied him to a meeting in Paris with European business leaders. The trip featured a sleepless Atlantic flight, followed immediately by meetings at the Ritz Hotel and a long lunch soaked with champagne and wine, followed by more meetings. By this time, I was almost falling off my chair, but Javits remained wide awake and alert. Like Humphrey, who typically didn't go to bed until two in the morning, Javits could function well on a few hours of sleep.

For decades, the Senate had been a deeply conservative body, dominated by Southern Democrats, but by the time I went to work for Humphrey, the chamber's makeup was turning younger and more liberal. Humphrey held a key Senate role—deputy majority leader behind Senator Mike Mansfield of Montana, with whom he had a strong cooperative relationship. Mansfield was intelligent, but not assertive, and he was quite prepared to defer to Humphrey and the White House. Looking back, I realize that this period before Humphrey stepped into the vice presidency was probably a highlight of his career and likely eased some of the insecurity that resulted from his hardscrabble youth. When Congress was in session, he would join breakfast meetings every Tuesday morning in the White House with President Kennedy and his staff, going over assorted legislative matters.

Humphrey and Kennedy were not personally close. The two had similar policy views, though Kennedy was far more the cold warrior. But they had faced off in the 1960 presidential primary, and Kennedy's decisive upset victory in West Virginia had knocked Humphrey out of the race. Afterward, Humphrey resented the money the Kennedy family had poured into the contest, and he particularly disliked Bobby Kennedy, who had promoted the rumor that Humphrey had dodged service in World War II. (In fact, Humphrey had tried to enlist several times but was rejected for color blindness and other ailments. He worked stateside in war-related jobs.)

President Kennedy's reliance on Humphrey changed the dynamic between the two men. Humphrey enthusiastically supported the president's agenda, and Kennedy and his staff came to depend heavily on the senator. The relationship enhanced Humphrey's status in Washington, the country, and the world, and it nursed his eagerness to one day become president himself.

I helped prepare the senator for his meetings with the president, and I worked on other foreign policy issues of central importance to Humphrey, including Foreign Relations Committee work. President Kennedy had appointed Humphrey associates to run the new Arms Control and Disarmament Agency, the first unit in the executive branch focused strictly on reducing weapons of war. While Kennedy was alive, the agency successfully put arms control on the nation's agenda, a special interest of Humphrey's.

The senator's office was in the Russell Senate Office Building, and my interactions with him would vary considerably depending on his agenda. If he was to make a speech that I had a hand in writing, for example, I might confer with him several times a day for several days running. Similarly, we'd put in time together if an issue was before the Senate Foreign Relations Committee. But if he was away or at work on domestic issues, I might go a few days without speaking to him.

From the outset of his Senate career, Humphrey had taken an active interest in foreign affairs. In addition to his arms control concerns, he likewise focused on relations with the Soviet Union and the European allies of the United States. He took a strong role in the Food for Peace program, which sent surpluses of American grain—including wheat, barley, and oats from Minnesota farmers—to needy populations around the globe, much of it going to India.

The senator and I held similar liberal, internationalist views of the world. Though we would occasionally disagree on specific issues, he was invariably thoughtful and happy to talk through differences. He never got mad when I disagreed with him.

As I settled into the job, however, I found the quality of his staff to be mixed. There were some talented people—Norman Sherman, his press secretary; John Stewart, the legislative assistant; Douglas Bennett, a speechwriter; Ted Van Dyk, director of communications; and others. Humphrey himself was generous and loyal, but he was anything but a disciplinarian. The office was somewhat disorganized. And Humphrey tended to be influenced by the last person to whom he had spoken—a particularly dangerous weakness in Washington.

In 1959, before I joined the staff, Humphrey's top legislative aide, Tom Hughes, a brilliant former Rhodes Scholar, had left, feeling underappreciated and discouraged by the disorder in the office. Hughes had developed a close friendship with Chester Bowles, a former Connecticut governor and former ambassador to India. When Bowles won a U.S. House seat in 1958, he offered Hughes the job of administrative assistant. The job was attractive not simply as an escape from the Humphrey staff disorder. As the chief foreign policy advisor to John F. Kennedy's presidential campaign, Bowles was a likely candidate for Secretary of State if Kennedy won. I asked Hughes at one point why he would leave a prestigious position with an important senator to become an aide to a first-term congressman. Hughes replied, "Would you have any confidence in Bill Connell and Herb Waters?"—the two principal figures who would be running the Humphrey presidential campaign in 1960. (After the election, Kennedy appointed Bowles Under Secretary of State, though he was pushed out within a year, by some accounts because of his opposition to the Bay of Pigs invasion in Cuba. Hughes went on to become director of the State Department's Bureau of Intelligence and Research.)

Hughes once told me that in three years as Humphrey's legislative assistant in the Senate, he never once had lunch or dinner with Humphrey alone. Over time, I came to suspect that Humphrey did not fully appreciate well-educated, notably bright people—perhaps another legacy of his family's struggles and his interrupted education.

The Humphrey staff did not enjoy a robust reputation on Capitol Hill. Much of the problem stemmed from top aide Bill Connell, who considered himself a Renaissance man of politics and intruded into policy matters about which he knew little, such as foreign relations. Political reporters would occasionally fault Humphrey for not seeing Connell's limitations, but the senator maintained great confidence in him.

Connell's dislike for me surfaced quickly and remained even after we both had left the staff. Early on, someone came to me and asked to meet with Humphrey. I passed the request to Connell, who handled the senator's appointments; he told me the man was not important enough to waste the senator's time. I agreed and informed the individual, assuming that was the end of it. But apparently the man ran into Humphrey. As often happened, Humphrey invited him back to the office. Connell concluded that I had gone behind his back, and he admonished me in a vicious note.

I should have dealt with the problem then. I wouldn't go to Humphrey—he was intensely uncomfortable dealing with staff friction. But I should have confronted Connell. Instead, I suffered his continuing harassment. Years later—in 1979—long after Humphrey had left office, a biographer asked Connell to organize a meeting of the senator's previous foreign policy advisers for an information-gathering session. Connell included nine advisers—everyone but me, who had served six years in the role.

Humphrey's fellow Minnesota senator in those days was Eugene McCarthy, a man I admired. A Catholic and intellectual, McCarthy had written extensively on church-state relations, and I'd read his work with appreciation as I prepared to write my PhD thesis on that subject. At one point, while still at Harvard, I'd inquired about getting a job on his senate staff but was told there were no openings.

Humphrey and McCarthy enjoyed a warm friendship, but Humphrey was clearly the senior partner. He'd entered the Senate in 1949 and supported McCarthy when he entered the House of Representatives that year. When McCarthy ran for a Senate seat in 1958, Humphrey backed him, despite a close relationship with a rival for the nomination. McCarthy signed on as campaign co-chairman for Humphrey's 1960 run for president. Though McCarthy was more conservative on the economy, they agreed on most issues.

Their friendship survived an awkward period in 1964, when both were short-listed on President Lyndon Johnson's roster of potential running mates, and both men wanted the job. Johnson and McCarthy were not personally close, but McCarthy's wife, Abigail, was a close friend of Lady Bird Johnson, which McCarthy hoped might give him an advantage, according to Humphrey's biographer Arnold A. Offner.[3] After a drawn-out period of suspense, Johnson named Humphrey at almost the last minute, and McCarthy put Humphrey's name in nomination at the Democratic convention in Atlantic City.

I didn't come to know McCarthy during my Washington years, to my regret, but that's hardly surprising—he had little regard for Congressional staffers, his own or those working for others. He had a weak staff and used it badly or not at all. He wrote his own speeches and articles. As a senator, he didn't care about constituent services, so most of them fell to the staff of the other Minnesota senator, Hubert Humphrey.

McCarthy was one of the foremost intellectuals in Congress. He had entered the House two years after John Kennedy, and early on the two Irish Catholics became close. McCarthy's personal secretary in those days was Mary Cram, the wife of McCarthy's close friend from St. John's University, Cleve Cram. Mary Cram told me that Kennedy would come often to McCarthy's office to discuss issues, and McCarthy did most of the talking. He'd long been studying and writing about key public concerns, while Kennedy's thinking was still largely unformed; he was spending time chasing girls together with his friend George Smathers, a congressman and later senator from Florida. When Kennedy entered the Senate in 1953, the meetings with McCarthy fell away.

McCarthy was widely assumed to believe that the first Irish

---

3 Offner, Arnold A., *Hubert Humphrey*, Yale University Press (2018), p. 194.

Catholic president should be Gene McCarthy, not Jack Kennedy. He supported Humphrey in the 1960 primary and at the last minute backed Adlai Stevenson at the Democratic convention that year with a rousing nominating speech, an act that angered the Kennedy circle and ensured McCarthy's exclusion from Camelot, though he did eventually endorse Kennedy.

McCarthy's brilliance had a coldness to it, some would say an arrogance. He had enormous confidence in his own ideas and analytical abilities, a certitude reflected in his failure to use his staff and in his dismissive attitude in later years toward most of his Senate colleagues. The arrogance seemed to inflate after his run for the presidency in 1968. He hardly acknowledged the thousands of young people who had worked on his campaign, many leaving school to pitch in. He later left his wife and continued to run unsuccessfully for the presidency.

The two fellow Minnesotans, McCarthy and Humphrey, remained collegial in the first years after Humphrey became vice president, but their opposing views on the Vietnam War later pulled them apart. During the 1968 Nixon-Humphrey presidential race, McCarthy waited until the election was only 10 days away before giving a tepid endorsement of Humphrey. Some fervent Humphrey supporters argued that with an earlier McCarthy endorsement, Humphrey would have won. In any case, as much as McCarthy had been an early hero of mine, I came to realize that Hubert Humphrey was a far better human being.

On November 22, 1963, I was in Sao Paulo, Brazil, subbing for Senator Humphrey at an OAS conference. I'd spent the day locked down in my hotel room, writing a speech to be delivered that night at another private conference. After finishing a draft, I climbed into a taxi at around 5:00 that afternoon to go to the conference venue. The taxi driver gave me a newspaper with the huge headline, "Kennedy Mataran" (Kennedy Killed). The conference was called off, and I wandered aimlessly. I cried as I had never cried as an adult, and to this day I regard the assassination of JFK as the saddest day of my life. While walking, I encountered two friends, also in Sao Paulo for the conference: Sergio Ossa, who would go on to be a close adviser to Chile's next president, and Monsignor Joseph Gremillion, an American who worked closely with Humphrey in the Food for Peace program. They and others expressed their condolences and their shock at Kennedy's death.

I ended up traveling from Rio to Washington on the same flight as the Brazilian and Argentine delegations to the Kennedy funeral. My wife, our children, and I joined the millions to view the Kennedy cortege. Robert Kennedy later asked me to conduct the Brazil portion of the Kennedy Oral History Project.

Despite wide differences in style, outlook, and geographic background, the new, unelected president, Lyndon Baines Johnson, had a history of working closely with Senator Humphrey. As a Texas senator, Johnson had calculated that if he wanted to reach the presidency, he needed a profile as a national leader, not as a Southern politician. He picked the amenable, liberal Minnesotan as an ally in that quest, and the two collaborated on assorted legislative initiatives. When Johnson left the Senate to become vice president, he arranged to have Humphrey appointed deputy majority leader.

Their relationship deepened after LBJ became president. Johnson sought Senator Humphrey's advice on a wide variety of issues, and Humphrey was often at the White House in meetings. Johnson arranged to have Humphrey lead the administration's most significant domestic initiative, the civil rights bill. After a long Senate filibuster, it passed in June 1964. Humphrey, who knew he was on the list of potential vice presidential selections, had complete confidence in Johnson's ability to govern well.

Still, a first wrinkle appeared just 11 days after the Kennedy assassination. As vice president, Johnson had not been involved with the Alliance for Progress, yet he knew Humphrey had been a key supporter of the program. The new president asked Humphrey to give him a memo on the Alliance and on policy toward Latin America. The senator mentioned the request to me, and we started thinking about putting something together. A few days later, at 8:00 on a Saturday morning, Johnson called Humphrey at home asking for that Alliance for Progress memo. Humphrey called me and I rushed into the office and together we started cobbling a document. At a little after noon, Johnson called again: "Where's that memo?"

We scurried to finish, with Humphrey assembling pages as they came out of the copier. He then rushed in a limousine up to the White House and was immediately ushered into the Oval Office. Johnson was there, but so was another man, Thomas Mann—a conservative Texan and longtime Foreign Service officer who had served as assistant secretary of state for Latin America in the Eisenhower administration. Now, Mann was ambassador to Mexico, a role that had led to a close acquaintance with his fellow Texan Johnson.

As Humphrey explained to me later, Mann's presence set off immediate warning signals, but Johnson urged Humphrey to go ahead and read the memo. Of course, the memo we had written aggressively supported Kennedy's Alliance for Progress and strongly recommended keeping in place the key people who were running it. As he read, Humphrey could see Mann fidgeting and looking nervous, but when the reading concluded, Johnson enthused about various points we'd made and indicated that he was going to follow Humphrey's advice.

In fact, Johnson had no interest in the Alliance for Progress; he basically disagreed with it. For one, he didn't like many of the American liberals who were behind the program. And though he'd become a reformer on a portfolio of domestic issues, he believed in keeping the status quo in Latin America.

After registering his enthusiasm, Johnson dropped the other shoe: He told Humphrey that in 15 minutes he was going down to the press room to announce that he was appointing Tom Mann assistant secretary of state and the coordinator of the Alliance for Progress. Mann would be the czar for Latin America. And the president told Humphrey to join him for the announcement and then tell the press why he supported the appointment.

Humphrey was in a bind. He was wary of Mann, but he knew that before long Johnson would pick his running mate. So the senator did as he was told.

Soon after, Johnson fired all the top Kennedy people running the Alliance for Progress. Within a month of the assassination, they were gone.

Word quickly got out around Latin America that a conservative Republican was now in charge of the Alliance, and the program was essentially dead. Over the next year, various Latin American officials who'd been involved in the Alliance would come to Washington. They'd pay a courtesy call on Mann, but then visit Humphrey's office to talk to the senator and me. Soon enough, even those visits died off as it became clear that Humphrey had no influence in the matter.

Humphrey and I made one last effort in defense of the program. As I described in the opening to this book, we wrote an article for the July 1964 issue of the magazine *Foreign Affairs*. The article, "U.S. Policy in Latin America," bylined Hubert H. Humphrey, vigorously defended the Alliance and Kennedy's policy in Latin America. The Alliance, we wrote, "is designed to abolish the shocking economic and social inequality, between privileged and impoverished, between glittering capitals and festering slums, between booming industrial regions and primitive rural areas. The Alliance is designed to be a peaceful alternative to violent revolution in meeting the challenge of an unjust socio-economic order."

In language that disgruntled Mann and certainly must have annoyed Johnson, if he saw it, we said, "President Kennedy himself was the symbol of the Alliance, the symbol of the hope and imagination which is needed. He realized that though Latin America faces grave economic problems, these must be seen within a broader political context. It is not just a matter of satisfying physical needs and raising material standards of living. What is more important is the problem of inspiring hope, of commanding the intellectual and emotional allegiance of those who will shape the society—both the élite groups and the popular classes."

We went on to point out that the U.S. commitment should go beyond providing assistance; it should also set a moral example. Given Latin America's large nonwhite population, we said, the United States needed to reform itself—"achieving equality for the Negro" and elevating "our attitude to our fellow citizens in the hemisphere." And we concluded by repeating Kennedy's description of Latin America as "the most critical area in the world."

The magazine itself and articles about the article circulated widely in the region. I heard that Mann was furious and told a confidant that I was behind the essay. But he was always quite proper with me, and he knew Humphrey was on Johnson's short list for vice president. The Alliance petered out, and soon enough, Vietnam eclipsed virtually all other foreign policy issues.

If Johnson hadn't pulled the plug, could the Alliance for Progress have made a difference in the progress of democracy in Latin America? I think unquestionably yes. American financial aid to Latin

America dropped precipitously—from more than $7 billion (in 2019 dollars) in the mid-1960s to less than $2 billion just over 10 years later, according to a 2022 report from the Congressional Research Service. Today, aid hovers at around $3 billion. Beyond money, knowledge of an American president's backing served as powerful support for reformist leaders across the region. When that went away, the traditional power centers stayed in control in most countries, and the window for widespread economic and social change during that era essentially closed.

Working with Humphrey and following developments in South America after Humphrey's defeat in 1968, I gained a chilling picture of the impact of changing American policy—a descent from the Alliance for Progress to President Richard Nixon's sharp turn against support for reform. Today, the sorry impact of that descent is still felt in many struggling countries of Latin America.

As 1964 unfolded, Humphrey was occupied with a range of President Johnson's projects, particularly the civil rights bill, but the senator continued to keep track of events in South America, which he had visited and where he continued to have friends. One event in particular drew our attention: A vital election was coming up that September in Chile, a country that became the focus of Washington's interest.

Among Latin American countries, Chile stood out for its robust history of democratic tradition. It featured a parliamentary government and a multiparty system. The country's 11 million people were urbanized and overwhelmingly literate. Chilean women had long held the right to vote. And Chile had been a focus of the Alliance for Progress, receiving millions in aid, more than any other country in the region.

But Washington was worried about the upcoming 1964 election for Chilean president. The Social Democratic candidate, Salvador Allende, a Marxist, was running in a coalition with the Communist Party of Chile along with several smaller leftist parties. Though Allende believed in the democratic process, U.S. officials thought that if elected, he wouldn't be able to control his militant coalition partner, the Communists, who, it was assumed, would undermine democratic traditions. This was just a few years after Fidel Castro introduced communist rule to Cuba—so far, the only Latin American country to embrace that ideology. Washington was deeply fearful that communism would spread in the hemisphere, and it was known that the Soviet Union was pouring money into the Allende candidacy.

What's more, several American companies had extensive interests in Chile, including Kennecott Copper and Anaconda Copper, both of which owned copper mines, and International Telephone and Telegraph (ITT), which operated communications systems. Allende was on record in favor of nationalizing major industries, and the American businesses were anxious.

As 1964 began, two candidates stood against Allende, and U.S. officials were divided on which to support. The more conservative was Julio Duran, who ran with a coalition of center-right parties and had the backing of Tom Mann and the American ambassador to Chile, the former Amherst College president Charles Cole. The centrist candidate was Christian Democrat Eduardo Frei, whose American supporters included Desmond Fitzgerald, head of the Latin American division of the CIA, as well as two other key American figures in Santiago, the CIA station chief and the deputy chief of mission at the embassy. Humphrey supported Frei and let President Johnson know it.

In a local election that spring, a conservative candidate backed by Julio Duran lost badly, prompting Duran to drop out of the presidential race. At that point, American support coalesced behind Frei, and Washington decided to back his campaign. The CIA provided money and other support, including polling, propaganda and organizing assistance.

It's worth stepping back for a moment to provide some context to the CIA's actions. After World War II, while the Cold War dominated international relations, the CIA used covert means to influence the internal politics in a number of countries. For the most part, this involved money and other logistic support, though in some instances—Iran and Guatemala, for example—it went far beyond that. President Dwight Eisenhower endorsed covert action because, for one thing, it was far cheaper than outright military intervention. During his long tenure as CIA director, Allan Dulles relentlessly advocated covert action.

At the same time, the Soviet Union was itself pouring money and effort into revolutionary struggles around the globe. With the Cold War raging, it made sense for the United States to counter the Soviet moves. This was frequently done through the CIA, but the agency operated in near secrecy. Only the president and the highest reaches of the executive branch knew what the CIA was up to—and in several cases, the CIA operations proved badly misguided, the fiasco with the Cuban Bay of Pigs invasion being the most notorious.

In 1975, the Senate's Church Committee exposed an alarming portfolio of CIA wrongdoing, from spying on American citizens to plotting to assassinate foreign leaders. Though several of the Church Committee's staff reports remain classified to this day, the Committee released one titled "Covert Action in Chile 1963-1973," which documented extensive agency operations. "The 1964 presidential election was the most prominent example of a large-scale election project," the report said. "The Central Intelligence Agency spent more than $2.6 million in support of the election of the Christian Democratic candidate, in part to prevent the accession to the presidency of Marxist Salvador Allende. More than half of the Christian Democratic candidate's campaign was financed by the United States...." In addition, the CIA station in Santiago "furnished support to an array of pro-Christian Democratic student, women's, professional and peasant groups."

Humphrey knew generally that American aid was being channeled to Eduardo Frei through the CIA, and he welcomed the provision of appropriate financial support. But because of agency secrecy, Humphrey had no idea whether the level of support for Frei was sufficient. In May 1964, he asked me how I thought our friends in Chile were getting on. I said I did not know for certain. So the senator suggested that I go to Chile and check out the situation on the ground.

I flew to Santiago and talked with a wide range of people, including Sergio Ossa, the friend I had encountered in Sao Paulo after the Kennedy assassination. Presidential candidate Eduardo Frei left his son's soccer game on a Sunday afternoon to receive me at his home. His English was not good, and my Spanish was not fluent, so I brought Guillermo Videla, a friend of Frei, as an interpreter. Frei was cordial and said he was pleased with how things were going; key people in his campaign told me the same thing. Rumors floated in the Chilean press that if Allende won, the military would stage a coup and oust him. But I came across no evidence of that, and the Church Committee later confirmed that Washington was not part of any coup planning around the 1964 election.

When I returned, I wrote a memorandum for Humphrey that he circulated to Secretary of State Dean Rusk and National Security Advisor McGeorge Bundy. One of them must have sent it to the CIA because an assistant to Des Fitzgerald, the Latin America CIA chief, called to ask if I would be willing to brief several CIA officers on what I knew. Two CIA officers came to my home for a 90-minute talk.

It turned out that Frei won the election handily with 57% of the vote, and he embarked on a program of reforms.

Shortly after the election, the CIA called again, and I was invited to meet Des Fitzgerald. We had lunch in a handsome CIA house in the Georgetown neighborhood of Washington. (Whether or not the house was supposed to be secret, many people in Washington knew of it.) Fitzgerald and I hit it off. We met several times again, and after Fitzgerald became director of covert operations worldwide, I arranged for him to meet with Humphrey when he served as vice president.

The father of the journalist Frances FitzGerald, who wrote the acclaimed 1972 book *Fire in the Lake* about the Vietnam War, Fitzgerald was trained as a lawyer at Harvard. He was one of several senior officials of the CIA whom I came to know during my time in Washington. They struck me as astute and well-meaning, though this was before accounts of the agency's many abuses surfaced.

In late 1967, Fitzgerald, as covert operations chief, briefed Secretary of Defense Robert McNamara. Fitzgerald's analysis of the Vietnam situation was unreservedly pessimistic. McNamara seemed surprised and asked, "Do you really think it is that bad, Des?"

"Yes, I do," Des responded. He never briefed McNamara again.[4]

As for Chile, Frei's reform efforts met resistance from conservative Chilean lawmakers, while his liberal supporters pushed for more action. The reformist president was caught in the middle, and the country grew more polarized. Under Chilean law, Frei served for six years, but he couldn't run for two consecutive terms. In the 1970 election, Allende was again a candidate of the far left, opposed by a left-wing Christian Democrat, Radmiro Tomic, and a conservative candidate. By then, Richard Nixon was president, and he dramatically changed American policy, favoring a more aggressive anti-communist approach to Latin America.

---

4 Thomas, Evan, *The Very Best Men*, Simon & Schuster (1995), p. 286.

Allende won a plurality in the first stage of Chile's 1970 election, but because he didn't win a majority, the final vote needed to be ratified by the Chilean Congress. Nixon was horrified at the prospect of an Allende victory, not least because of what that would mean to major American businesses operating in Chile. So Nixon ordered a reluctant CIA Director Richard Helms to make sure Allende didn't win in Congress; if that didn't work, Nixon made clear he wanted the CIA to help arrange a military coup.

The coup effort at that point never materialized, and Allende won the second round of the election and became Chile's president. The White House was distraught. According to the Church Committee report, Nixon's National Security advisor, Henry Kissinger, told the press in a background briefing that a communist government in Chile could create a domino effect in South America, with the risk that Argentina, Peru, and Bolivia would turn communist.

As Allende's administration carried on, the CIA worked with a group of Chilean military officers to arrange a coup. On September 11, 1973, a military junta led by General Augusto Pinochet staged a coup, taking over the government and establishing a dictatorship. During the takeover, Allende shot himself with an AK-47 in the presidential palace.

The Church Committee report says it found no evidence that the United States was involved directly in the coup. Indeed, the report suggests that the CIA was plotting with a different group of officers than the Pinochet junta. However, the report establishes that the agency supplied enormous support in money, propaganda, and logistical aid to efforts to disrupt and destabilize the Allende government.

The repressive Pinochet regime, known for torturing and murdering political opponents, remained in power until 1990 before democracy finally returned to the Latin American country with one of the region's richest democratic traditions.

The Chilean election in 1964 was just one example of an aggressive American intervention in foreign elections during the Cold War—a historical record that lends a taint of hypocrisy to outrage over the Russian meddling in the 2016 election in our country. Some officials maintain that the United States eliminated or considerably curtailed the practice after the Church Committee findings and the later demise of the Soviet Union.[5] I assume that if the U.S. intervenes now, it does so less often and in a much less intrusive way. But the story of the U.S. meddling in Chile under Nixon and Kissinger adds another unhappy note to the history of America's treatment of its southern neighbors.

---

5 Goldsmith, Jack, "Does the U.S. Still Interfere in Foreign Elections," October 28, 2020, *Project Syndicate*.

CHAPTER 5
VIETNAM RISING

Like most Americans, I was only casually aware of Vietnam in the early 1960s.

In the aftermath of World War II, American foreign policy had sporadically focused on Southeast Asia. The Soviet Union's aggression in the years just after the war drew the attention of the United States primarily toward Europe and the Near East and led to the creation of NATO and to the Truman Doctrine, declared by President Harry Truman in 1947. Under that principle, for the first time, it became American policy to offer military and economic support to democratic regimes under threat from authoritarian aggression, both internal and external. As the State Department's Office of Historian puts it, "The Truman Doctrine effectively reoriented U.S. foreign policy, away from its usual stance of withdrawal from regional conflicts not directly involving the United States, to one of possible intervention in far away conflicts."

The communist takeover in China and the Korean War pulled American attention to the East, and many American experts worried about a "domino theory"—the notion that if one country fell to the communists, others would fall in turn. Southeast Asia became a particular focus of concern. Vietnam was a French colony, and the French at the time were battling an insurgency led by Ho Chi Minh, an acknowledged Marxist. For the United States, the situation pitted two policies against each other: avowed opposition to colonialism and containment of the spread of communism.

The French made a military last stand against Ho's insurgents at a site called Dien Bien Phu, and as the battle turned against the colonizers, the French sought military help from President Dwight Eisenhower. When America's traditional allies refused to join in rescuing the French, Eisenhower said no. The French capitulated, and in a 1954 conference in Geneva, Vietnam was divided into separate countries, North and South, with vague future plans for reunification.

The conflict between communists and noncommunists, though muted for a time, continued, and the Viet Cong increasingly harassed the forces of the unpopular South Vietnamese president Ngo Dinh Diem. Eisenhower and Kennedy, both believers in the domino theory, sent advisers and significant financial aid, but both presidents were wary of committing troops.

Though the conflict festered while I was at the State Department, I heard little about it. After I moved to Senator Humphrey's staff, questions about Vietnam started coming up, and I sensed from talking with the senator that he would oppose any expansion of the American role. The assassination—with American complicity—of the autocratic South Vietnamese President Diem in a military coup in November 1963 sharply focused American attention on Vietnam, but the Kennedy assassination soon captured the news.

Starting in early 1964, however, more discussions of Southeast Asia came up in the Senate and the media. Several senators—Frank Church of Idaho, Wayne Morse of Oregon, and Ernest Gruening of Alaska, among them—spoke out against further U.S. involvement. President Kennedy had raised the number of noncombat American advisers in South Vietnam from around 6,000 to around 16,000, but the Viet Cong continued to make inroads. Lyndon Johnson, who'd assumed the presidency following Kennedy's assassination, knew that sending troops to Vietnam would be unpopular in that election year, so he said early on that there would be no escalation of the American commitment. He famously talked about letting Asian boys fight Asian wars. Throughout 1964, he essentially maintained Kennedy's policy, simply sending over a few thousand more advisers.

At the same time, a noisy faction of conservatives—among them

Republican Senator Barry Goldwater of Arizona—argued that American foreign policy was weak against communism. There was frequent talk of the domino theory. And some top American military commanders, prominently Curtis LeMay, chief of staff of the Air Force, called for an aggressive military response in Vietnam.

From his years on the Senate Foreign Relations Committee, Humphrey had stayed aware of the events unfolding in Southeast Asia, and he occasionally spoke out about the region in the Senate. A strong anticolonialist, he criticized the French for failing to give independence to Vietnam. But like so many others of his time, he held to the domino theory, at least through the 1950s and early 1960s. His opinions became more nuanced as the South Vietnamese government floundered badly and as public discussion of Vietnam increased. He also came to know the views of Major General Edward Lansdale, a former CIA officer and counterinsurgency expert who had spent years in Vietnam. Lansdale maintained that success in Vietnam depended on social and political reforms and effective counterinsurgency methods, not full-scale military intervention.

With the talk heating up, I started researching the situation, reading books and commentaries pro and con and talking to knowledgeable people, including Jim Thomson, on the staff of National Security Adviser McGeorge Bundy, and the former Humphrey staffer Tom Hughes, now head of intelligence and research and in Dean Rusk's State Department. I wanted to write a memo for Humphrey giving background and options, and I quickly found those arguing against escalation far more persuasive. In addition to Thomson and Hughes, these included political scientists, such as Hans Morgenthau of the University of Chicago, and journalists, such as Walter Lippmann, the dean of columnists, and Joseph Kraft, whose Washington-based column was widely syndicated. Even Charles de Gaulle, the president of France, was cautioning against a commitment of American troops.

My research indicated that the domino theory was flawed. It defied history. North Vietnam had been ruled by a communist government for more than a decade, and other countries hadn't followed. Whether a particular nation turned communist had much more to do with its internal situation than with what was happening in neighboring countries. This was particularly true where the conflict was a guerrilla war, essentially a political struggle in which the outcome depended largely on the support of the people. "Americanizing" the conflict in Vietnam—sending in U.S. troops to supplant the feckless South Vietnamese army—as was being suggested in some quarters, would be counterproductive. The French experience showed that the populace was unlikely to support Western soldiers fighting Vietnamese nationals, regardless of the ideology at play.

On June 8, 1964, I gave Humphrey a nine-page memo outlining points and recommendations. I explained that I wanted to give the senator some policy alternatives in case he was drawn into a discussion of Vietnam. But I urged him not to make a speech on the subject or send a memo on Vietnam to the president.

Why? I didn't say it in the memo, though I strongly suspected given what I knew of LBJ that the president quietly favored a more aggressive American approach than did Humphrey (or I). An outspoken embrace of a dovish policy could torpedo Humphrey's coveted chance to be picked as Johnson's running mate. At the same time, I warned the senator against being maneuvered into publicly defending the administration's current policy against Senate critics such as Church, Morse, and Gruening. Better to stay aloof from the issue for the time being.

I went on to offer some points to consider in the event Humphrey was drawn into a discussion. My first concerned America's overall objectives in Vietnam. I agreed with President Kennedy's observation that the United States was overcommitted in Southeast Asia, particularly in the context of America's wider foreign policy obligations. I continued, "The problem is how to correct this imbalance in our commitments without impairing our own prestige and without weakening and embarrassing non-Communist friends and allies in that area. There should be no question of an abrupt withdrawal from the Indo-China peninsula, or specifically from the country currently most vulnerable, South Viet-Nam." Our objective, I said, "is to withdraw from the area gradually and gracefully and in a way that would not leave South Viet-Nam vulnerable to Communist domination from the North. What we are after therefore is _not_ 'victory,' but a stable political settlement."

I pointed out the likely futility of sending American troops to fight, quoting Secretary of Defense Robert McNamara that the conflict "is a counter-guerrilla war, it is a war that can only be won by the Vietnamese themselves." (Frustrated at the lack of success in Vietnam, McNamara would soon become an advocate of sending in

American troops.)

Extending the war to the North with bombs or raids presented a different set of problems, I wrote, though people both in the Johnson administration and out were calling for that more aggressive approach. For one thing, that likely wouldn't deter the Viet Cong, the guerrilla force opposing the Diem regime; the Viet Cong were by now well established in the South and had the arms and support to sustain themselves for a long period of time. For another, I argued that attacking the North risked provoking either the Soviet Union or China to retaliate. The danger of intervention by China, which had a formal treaty with North Vietnam, seemed particularly acute and would have devastating consequences internationally and at home. (On this point, my concerns never materialized—despite American escalation, neither China nor the Soviet Union ever responded militarily.)

I suggested exploring the idea of sending some threatening signals to the North, such as stationing an aircraft carrier within sight of the North Vietnamese mainland or flying aircraft along the border. I speculated that the saber-rattling might pressure the North Vietnamese to negotiate without provoking the Soviets or China. I also suggested dangling a carrot to North Vietnam—the possibility of trade with South Vietnam. The North needed food, and the South could supply it.

As for potential negotiation with the North, I wrote, "we should never let our policymakers forget that our objective is an acceptable political settlement, not military victory. Emphasis on military 'victory' converts what is a means into an end." An acceptable settlement would mean most of the countries of Indochina would follow a nonaligned policy. China might not like that, I wrote, but might well tolerate it if those same countries were no longer client states of the United States or some other foreign power.

Above all, I emphasized, we should not send large numbers of new fighting troops to South Vietnam. "The reason is that once in it is very difficult to get these troops out. Here it seems to me that MacArthur's advice was sound, that we should not get involved in a land war in Asia."

Humphrey was pleased with the memo and didn't dissent from any point. Following my advice, he never shared it with Johnson.

Throughout that summer, the senator worked assiduously to advance LBJ's ambitious domestic agenda. The Civil Rights Act passed Congress in July, and Johnson's Great Society program—a portfolio of initiatives aimed at reducing poverty, advancing health care, reviving cities, aiding education, and generally improving the lives of Americans—was on the table. Meantime, Johnson had not announced his selection of a vice presidential running mate as the days ticked down to the Democratic National Convention in August.

Humphrey was widely considered a front-runner, but one cause of Johnson's hesitation about him was said to be the senator's well-established proclivity to talk too much. Johnson himself loved to tell stories, but he played his political strategy close to the vest. The president worried that Humphrey's garrulousness could lead to trouble. I'd already seen examples of the senator's verbosity—he'd deliver a 30-minute written speech and then add half an hour of extraneous remarks. His wife, Muriel, used to advise him before he stepped on the platform, "Remember, Hubert, to be immortal you don't have to be eternal." But it usually didn't do any good.

In the lead-up to the convention and then in the campaign, however, Humphrey was very guarded in conversation. He didn't want a comment to leak that would irritate the president.

At some point that summer, Johnson asked Humphrey to deliver a speech on Vietnam—the president presumably wanted a figure who commanded respect from liberals to speak on behalf of administration policy. To help write the speech, I enlisted the Bundy staffer Jim Thomson, who was an Asia expert, and Bryce Nelson, a foreign policy assistant to Senator Frank Church, a close friend of Humphrey's.

Thomson wrote the first draft, and I edited it. We both understood the importance of not deviating from the current American policy of an advisory-only role, and the speech we produced was anodyne. Humphrey delivered it and hardly anyone noticed. Not many papers even covered it.

Early in August, two U.S. Navy patrol boats covertly gathering electronic intelligence in the Gulf of Tonkin, near North Vietnamese territorial waters, purportedly came under attack from the North

Vietnamese. (American officials later acknowledged that the supposed attack on the second boat hadn't happened.) Johnson used the incidents to ask Congress for a resolution authorizing him "to take all necessary measures to repel an armed attack" and "to prevent further aggression" by North Vietnam. The president selected Senator William Fulbright of Arkansas—later a prominent critic of the war—to shepherd the resolution through Congress, and it flew through, passing the House unanimously and drawing only two dissents in the Senate, from Morse and Gruening.

I don't recall any serious discussion with Humphrey about the merits of the resolution. People generally accepted the official American explanation of the incidents and rallied around the flag. Within the Senate, the fact that Senator Fulbright supported the resolution counted for a lot—he was highly respected and was known to be skeptical of escalating American actions. At the time, neither Humphrey nor I realized the impact of the measure—it allowed Johnson to expand America's commitment into a full-fledged war without any further congressional approval.

With the Democratic National Convention coming up in late August in Atlantic City, Bill Connell drew up the list of Humphrey aides who were to accompany the senator, and, continuing his antagonism, he excluded me. But I wasn't about to miss out on this important event, where I expected my boss to be nominated for the vice presidency. So I booked a room and went to Atlantic City myself and participated in all the regular staff meetings. (Connell never said a thing.)

Johnson's nomination was a foregone conclusion, but he tried to inject some drama into the convention by waiting to name a running mate and playing the various contenders against each other. Humphrey grew frantic. Eugene McCarthy got fed up with being used in LBJ's machinations and withdrew his name from contention. Then LBJ dangled the possibility of picking Senator Tom Dodd of Connecticut. Finally, the day before Johnson was scheduled to announce his choice to the convention, he told Humphrey he had the job. By Humphrey's account, Johnson warned that he expected unswerving loyalty—a loyalty Humphrey had already pledged as Johnson sorted through candidates.

Humphrey celebrated with a rousing acceptance speech. To the intense delight of the Democratic delegates, he lambasted Barry

Goldwater, the Republican presidential nominee, insisting he was dangerously out of step with the American people and calling him the "temporary Republican spokesman." The senator ran down a litany of recent legislative accomplishments that were supported in the Senate by both Democrats and Republicans, finishing each mention with the refrain, "But *not* Senator Goldwater." After each, the delegates laughed and cheered wildly.

I was on the convention floor and thoroughly enjoyed the commotion. Afterward, at a celebratory party for Humphrey supporters, I saw Adlai Stevenson standing alone at the bar. I had met Stevenson several times, so I walked over to say hello, and my strongest recollection of the party was Stevenson's enormous relief to have some company. Most politicians dislike being alone. As John Bartlow Martin points out in his biography, *Adlai Stevenson and the World*, the former Illinois governor and two-time presidential candidate really hated it.[6]

Following the convention, the Johnson team floated the notion in the press that as vice president, Humphrey would play a key role in foreign policy in the Johnson administration. Accordingly, during the campaign that fall, the senator gave a series of speeches on leading foreign policy fronts. By then, Jim Thomson and Bryce Nelson had been officially deputized to help me, and the three of us prepared the talks with an informal task force—outside experts, such as Zbigniew Brzezinski, then at Columbia University, and various Kennedy appointees still in government, including Tom Hughes. The topics ranged from relations with China to arms control to NATO policy. We were careful not to push any hot-button issues, and Humphrey delivered each with little impact.

I'd come to know Tad Szulc, one of the chief foreign correspondents at *The New York Times,* and he asked if Humphrey would be willing to sit for an interview. I checked, and the senator agreed. He ended up talking to Szulc for several hours, outlining what would presumably be the administration's approach to international relations. Humphrey emphasized several times that the global communist threat was not monolithic—by then, China and the Soviet Union were at odds—and he talked about communism being "fragmented." Regarding conflicts in Southeast Asia, Humphrey said the solution

---

6 Martin, John Bartlow, *Adlai Stevenson and the World*, Doubleday (1977), p. 447.

should be regional, featuring the participation of India and Pakistan. With Vietnam in particular, he argued that the struggle was as much social and political as military, and the primary response should remain with the Vietnamese. "We should not attempt to take over the war from the Vietnamese," he said.

The long story appeared on the paper's front page on Sunday, September 13. The top story on the page that day described yet another coup in leadership in Saigon.

By election day, the results were a foregone conclusion. I watched the returns come in at a big party at a Minneapolis hotel. Afterward, Humphrey treated his staff and their spouses to several days at Caneel Bay in the Virgin Islands. Elizabeth joined me, and we had a lovely time. I'm sure she appreciated the break. By then we had three children—the two girls, Mary Ellen and Catherine, had been joined by a boy, Tom. A second son, John, would be born a year later. Elizabeth was thrilled that Humphrey had been elected and that I would be on the staff of the vice president of the United States.

I was pleased, too, and I entered 1965 with great expectations for the years ahead. I generally had confidence in Johnson's decision-making, and I thought Humphrey as vice president would play a significant role. That, of course, turned out not to be the case. Humphrey and his staff had much less influence on American policy, both foreign and domestic, than when he served as senator. Johnson totally dominated the process and essentially shut Humphrey out from anything important.

As I look back, my most satisfying and successful years with Humphrey came when he was in the Senate and had both prestige and power. When he was vice president, not only did his role shrink, but Vietnam overwhelmed the foreign policy agenda. On that issue, I was totally opposed to Johnson's policy, but I went out of my way to avoid embarrassing the vice president and getting him in trouble with a president who was known to expect obedient allegiance from his subordinates.

CHAPTER 6
EXILED

With Humphrey's elevation to vice president, I moved my office from the Russell Senate Office Building to two offices. One was in the Old Executive Office Building (now the Eisenhower Executive Office Building), the big, ornate structure just west of the White House. My space was down the hall from the vice president (Walter Mondale, Jimmy Carter's vice president, would be the first to have an office in the West Wing). I spent most of my time there, but Secretary of State Dean Rusk had also made available an office in the State Department Building (now the Truman Federal Building), a 20-minute walk away in the Washington area known as Foggy Bottom. That office helped me keep in touch with State Department colleagues, so I'd occasionally work there, too.

Throughout the difficult years of Humphrey's vice presidency, two friends in the State Department kept me closely informed about what was going on behind the scenes. Both were opposed to an escalation of the war. One was Tom Hughes, with whom I'd meet every month or so. The other was Ben Read, the chief of staff to Dean Rusk and a close associate of Under Secretary of State George Ball, who himself lobbied internally against getting involved in a war in Asia.

As Johnson's inauguration on January 20 approached, Vietnam remained a time bomb of an issue. LBJ had insisted on no change in policy before the election, but once he won an overwhelming mandate from the voters, he felt free to explore his options. In late November, he called together key foreign policy advisers to discuss how to proceed. Humphrey was not included, but according to my notes—based, I think, on information from Ben Read—the meeting unfolded this way: Johnson went around the table asking each man for his thoughts. He started with Bill Bundy, McGeorge Bundy's older brother (and the husband of Dean Acheson's daughter), who had served in the CIA during the Korean War and now worked in Asian affairs at the State Department. Bundy recalled that his colleagues during the Korean War had agreed that the United States should never get involved in another land war in Asia.

Next, Johnson turned to Mac Bundy, who agreed with his brother. Dean Rusk, who had been an assistant secretary of state during the Korean War, also advised against a land war in Asia. Several or all of them recalled MacArthur's famous warning.

When the inquiry came around to Robert McNamara and members of the Joint Chiefs of Staff, however, LBJ got different advice. They recommended an escalation, including bombing the North and the introduction of American fighting troops.

Johnson didn't commit one way or another at that time, but, according to my notes, he strongly indicated that he favored an escalation. As he saw it, committing American troops was the only way to avoid the humiliating defeat of the noncommunist government in South Vietnam and the spread of communism throughout Southeast Asia. Later, he also spoke of the necessity of standing up to a "bully"—the memory of Munich still weighed heavily with him and so many others. Once the two Bundys and Rusk saw where LBJ was going, they quickly came around.

Humphrey and I also dealt with Vietnam in the days before Johnson's inauguration. In early January, Albert Fraleigh, a former officer of the U.S. Agency for International Development (AID) and an associate of Edward Lansdale, the American counterinsurgency expert, gave a presentation to Humphrey and Senator Fulbright. (I don't recall that Lansdale was at the meeting, though other Fraleigh colleagues were.) Fraleigh later prepared a memo summing up what I called the Lansdale analysis, as presented at the meeting.

Fraleigh and Lansdale were scathingly critical of the American effort in Vietnam and the American personnel in charge of the effort. They thought the U.S. intervention up to then had been weak and feckless, but they opposed an escalation that would send in thousands of combat troops. Rather, Fraleigh and Lansdale thought the United States needed a new team in Vietnam and a new approach, one that focused on strengthening the Vietnamese desire for freedom while quietly providing aid and encouragement in areas where they lacked expertise.

The Landsdale/Fraleigh prescription for accomplishing this turnaround included courting and instructing groups in South Vietnam that were anti-communist and motivated to work for a strong, free nation—the groups listed in the memo included students, religious organizations, political parties, and the intelligentsia. Under the Lansdale/Fraleigh approach, American advisers would guide the leaders of these anti-communist groups toward effective social, political and military goals and coax these leaders into substantive positions of authority in South Vietnam. What's more, the Americans would tutor the South Vietnamese in military tactics that had proven effective in other independent nations facing attack—a nod to Lansdale's success in helping the Philippine government turn back a communist insurrection.

Fraleigh and Lansdale thought the current American team overseeing Vietnam was hopelessly inadequate and in particular had little sophistication in psychological operations, a Lansdale specialty. That team, including then Ambassador Maxwell Taylor, should be removed, and Fraleigh helpfully supplied a long list of potential replacements—a roster that included Lansdale and Fraleigh.

In a memo to Humphrey several days after the meeting, I acknowledged that the Lansdale group made a number of valid criticisms, but I argued that the analysis is "based on a premise that is highly questionable."

I pointed out that the Lansdale analysis rested on the notion that "the most important thing to achieve success in Viet-Nam is what the **Americans** do rather than what the Vietnamese do.... It is assumed that if the Americans act properly and wisely then the situation will turn out all right. It further assumes that the Americans can inject the vital element of motivation from the outside, that this does not have to come from within Vietnamese society itself. This assumption seems to me highly dubious at best."

I advised Humphrey not to send the Fraleigh memo to President Johnson—memos have a tendency to circulate in government, and I doubted it was in Humphrey's "interest to circulate a memorandum which in effect repudiates the present team in Saigon and Washington." But I thought it was important for the president to hear the Lansdale analysis, so—defying my usual advice—I suggested that Humphrey present it to Johnson orally.

I don't think Humphrey ever did, but I sent the Fraleigh memo to several senators I thought might be interested, including George McGovern, who had started to have serious doubts about the war.

The opportunity for President Johnson to unleash an aggressive new policy in Vietnam arrived in early February, when the Viet Cong launched a mortar attack on an American base near Pleiku, about 300 miles north of Saigon. The attack killed nine Americans and wounded more than 100. At the time, Mac Bundy happened to be in Saigon assessing the situation, and he visited Pleiku and examined the bloody scene. He fired back a cable to Johnson, urging retaliation by bombing North Vietnam.

Johnson called a meeting of his National Security Council, the statutorily designated top advisers on matters of national security. By law, the vice president is included, but Humphrey was in Minneapolis and missed that meeting. Johnson didn't respond to the attack immediately but called a second meeting the next day, which Humphrey again missed.

Two days after the Pleiku attack, the Viet Cong bombed a hotel housing U.S. servicemen at Qui Nhon, on the coast 100 miles east of Pleiku. The explosion killed 23 Americans. By then, Johnson had decided to launch a sustained bombing attack on North Vietnam. It hadn't begun yet, and Johnson called another NSC meeting. This time Humphrey attended.

Again, Johnson sought opinions from those attending, and almost all agreed on the necessity of retaliatory bombing. Even George Ball went along, at least to the extent that he advised the president to respond with care to avoid a Soviet reaction. But when LBJ turned to Humphrey, the vice president spoke his mind.

I'd advised him not to. I knew enough about Johnson's personality and management style to assume that if Humphrey challenged Johnson in front of others, the president would be unforgiving. He could readily close out Humphrey from a significant role in any aspect of American policy. I didn't anticipate that Vietnam would turn into the disaster that it did, and I hoped that Humphrey could exercise influence in foreign policy issues around the globe. The vice president had said he understood, and he vowed to me, his family, and friends that he would never speak out on a policy dispute with President Johnson in the presence of a third person. At most, he would speak to LBJ alone.

But the discussion at the NSC meeting that day provoked Humphrey, and he argued passionately against bombing the North. He pointed out that Soviet Premier Alexei Kosygin was visiting Hanoi right then, and Humphrey asked, "What would be the reaction of the American government if an American president was visiting in Mexico City and the Soviet Union launched an attack on Mexico?" Humphrey went on at considerable length—as he was wont to do—about what a mistake it would be to begin bombing the North. He was primarily concerned about provoking the Soviets or China, but he also knew that military might would not solve the puzzle of Vietnam—that negotiation was the only possible route toward a resolution.

Adlai Stevenson, also at the meeting, agreed with Humphrey. But their argument didn't change Johnson's mind. McNamara, Bundy, Rusk, and others all agreed that a bombing reprisal was necessary, and soon American fighter bombers launched from carriers offshore started their attacks, an operation that evolved into continuing sorties under the name Rolling Thunder.

Humphrey didn't yet realize that he'd infuriated Johnson. After the NSC meeting, the vice president told me that he needed to meet privately with the president to discuss the implications of what was going on in Vietnam. That meeting never took place.

A few days later, Ben Read let me know that Johnson had called another meeting—not an NSC meeting—to continue the discussion on Vietnam policy. I asked Bill Connell, who handled Humphrey's schedule, if the vice president had been notified. Connell said he'd heard nothing. Ben Read let me know what happened next: Connell called Bromley Smith, executive secretary for the NSC. When Connell asked if the vice president should attend, Smith paused for a long moment and then told Connell to hold on—he'd get back to him shortly.

Smith then went to his boss, Mac Bundy, and asked if the vice president should attend. Bundy, who had a very sensitive political antenna, told Smith he'd get back to him with an answer.

So the national security adviser of the United States walked over to the Oval Office and told the president that there had been an inquiry from the vice president about whether he should attend the upcoming meeting. Johnson erupted: "God damn it, Mac, can't I have a meeting in this town without everyone knowing about it." He raged on about leaks for the next few minutes.

Needless to say, Humphrey did not attend.

For the next three years, Vietnam never came up at NSC meetings. Why? Because the vice president of the United States is a statutory member of the Council, and apparently Johnson wanted to freeze Humphrey out of any consideration of Vietnam policy. Instead, discussions of Vietnam were held at meetings of a smaller group that included the secretaries of defense and state, the chairman of the Joint Chiefs of Staff, the head of the CIA, and, from time to time, other selected officials. These meetings became known as the "Tuesday lunches."

When I realized what was happening, I got Humphrey's approval to make an inquiry with George Springsteen, special assistant to George Ball at the State Department. I was scheduled to see Springsteen on other business, and I thought I'd sound him out on whether he thought Ball would be interested in keeping in touch with Humphrey on Vietnam. After all, Humphrey and Ball were longtime friends and had quite similar views on the subject. But when I gingerly floated the idea with Springsteen, it immediately became clear that Ball had no desire to deal with Humphrey on Vietnam. The event confirmed my suspicions: Humphrey was on his way to becoming a leper in the Johnson administration.

(Ball was one of the few Johnson administration officials who could push back on Vietnam policy and still stay within Johnson's inner circle. Ball's secret? He would disagree with LBJ during the week and then go on the Sunday TV talk shows and support the war.)

Two overlapping incidents over the next two weeks showed the opposite directions in which Humphrey was being pulled. Earlier, he had tentatively agreed to be the opening speaker at a United Nations–endorsed "Pacem in Terris" conference. Inspired by an encyclical from Pope John XXIII, the conference was designed to explore ways to bring peace to the world. It had been organized in part by the Center for the Study of Democratic Institutions, run by an old Humphrey friend, Robert Maynard Hutchins, the former president of the University of Chicago.

This would be a major speech—the first Humphrey would deliver as vice president. As the date of the conference neared, Humphrey realized he should get clearance for giving the speech from Rusk and Johnson. Rusk told him to cancel. When Humphrey asked the president, however, Johnson said to go ahead, but have Rielly clear the content beforehand with Bundy.

With the help of several colleagues, including Richard Gardner, a Columbia Law School professor who had been deputy assistant secretary of state, I prepared a draft. Humphrey was scheduled to spend a weekend at a friend's lodge in Georgia, and the vice president suggested that I come along to go over the proposed text. So I flew down with him, we worked on the speech, and after a day I flew back, preparing for my meeting to go over the text with Bundy.

Meantime, Secretary Rusk had decided after the election that someone should keep Humphrey apprised of developments across the range of foreign policy issues. The secretary of state had the best interests at heart of both Humphrey and the country. Rusk recalled that Harry Truman had succeeded Franklin Roosevelt as president after the barest of contact with FDR and almost no knowledge of what was going on in foreign relations—a dangerous precedent Rusk wanted to avoid. So he assigned Tom Hughes, the former Humphrey aide and current deputy director of the State Department's Bureau of Intelligence and Research, to brief Humphrey every now and then on the latest developments.

The two had had trouble finding compatible times to meet, so Humphrey suggested that Hughes come down to Georgia that weekend, too. He arrived after I'd left, and he flew back with the vice president.

Hughes was a close associate of George Ball's, and he and Ball agreed on the dangers of escalating the American military commitment to Vietnam. Hughes knew that Humphrey shared their views. What's more, Hughes knew the direction Johnson was leaning—toward a major escalation, including sending combat troops. Hughes explained this to Humphrey and warned that time was running out—if the vice president was to have any influence in slowing down, let alone stopping, a massive expansion of the American role in Vietnam, he had to do it quickly. Humphrey understood. He advised Hughes to put his thoughts in a draft and send it to him. He would revise it and send it to the president.

Hughes made the case against Americanizing the conflict in a 1,700-word memo. The memo—Humphrey revised it only slightly—remains a prescient description of the dangers of escalation. "American wars have to be politically understandable by the American public," the memo stated. With Vietnam, the public would question why the country would risk World War III with China to salvage a chronically unstable South Vietnamese government.

The memo emphasized the nuclear peril of provoking China and the Soviet Union, but it also said that even short of such an outcome, sending combat troops would undermine American policies throughout the world, in particular, progress toward warmer relations with the Soviet Union and efforts toward arms control. Rather than a military escalation, the goal should be to develop a political track toward a negotiated settlement. "We should take the initiative on the political side and not end up being dragged to a conference as an unwilling participant."

What's more, the memo asserted, the politics were all wrong. Expanding the military commitment would be to adopt the myopic Republican approach, a development that would likely alienate liberal Democrats, independents, labor, and church groups. The administration's domestic agenda would be seriously impeded.

Hughes and Humphrey recognized the ego and vanity of the man to whom the memo was ultimately directed and took that into account. "The President is personally identified with, and admired for, political ingenuity," the memo said. "He will be expected to put all his great political sense to work now for international political solutions. People will be counting upon him to use on the world scene his unrivalled talents as a political leader."

The memo artfully captured Humphrey's opposition to escalation and remains today a celebrated marker of anti-war sentiment within the Johnson administration. When Tom Hughes died in January 2023, Fredrik Logevall, the acclaimed Harvard historian, told *The New York Times*, "I have my students read this memo. It's an amazing document."

Despite my advice, Humphrey had earlier passed along several Vietnam memos. Now, he ignored my advice again. In this case, the vice president didn't send the Hughes memo directly to Johnson;

instead, he gave it to Bill Moyers, a special assistant to the president. Moyers passed it to Johnson.

In his 2022 biography of Hughes, *The Last Gentleman*, Bruce Smith writes, "McGeorge Bundy said years later that the memo 'broke up' the relationship between president and vice president. The Johnson-Humphrey relationship, he said, 'went sour faster than any in the two-hundred-year history of the troubled relationships between presidents and their vice presidents.'"[7]

Meantime, I ventured over to McGeorge Bundy's office to go over Humphrey's Pacem in Terris speech. I hadn't known Bundy at Harvard, though, of course, I knew of him, and he had later thanked me for taking over his seminar when he left for the White House. When I was on Humphrey's staff, I dealt with him only occasionally (I would see more of him at the Ford Foundation). Bundy was a trim man of average height, though he seemed small standing next to his tall colleagues LBJ and McNamara. His round face, large glasses, and receding hairline gave him a slightly owlish appearance. With me in those days he was always cordial, but businesslike and efficient. When it came to choosing friends, Bundy selected men such as Isaiah Berlin, Walter Lippmann, and Dean Acheson.

The material in the speech was carefully written to be quite bland, praising Pope John XXIII, citing American efforts to ease tensions with the Soviet Union, pointing to the dangers of proliferating nuclear armaments. But the speech veered briefly toward Vietnam, and we had inserted three paragraphs of original proposals, including one calling for negotiations. Bundy passed quickly over the speech but paused when he came to the first of the three substantive paragraphs. "John," he told me, "that's a very interesting idea. Excellent formulation, but that's not U.S. policy." Then he crossed the paragraph out. He said essentially the same thing before crossing out the two other important paragraphs. The rest of the speech stood as written.

Humphrey delivered it to the Pacem in Terris convocation in the U.N. General Assembly Hall on February 17. Afterward, I rode up to a reception in an elevator with the vice president, U.N. Secretary-General U Thant, and William Benton, the CEO of Encyclopedia

---

[7] Smith, Bruce, *The Last Gentleman: Thomas Hughes and the End of the American Century*, Brookings Institution Press (2022), p. 2.

Britannica and a close friend and supporter of Humphrey's. When the elevator doors closed, Benton pounced. "Hubert, that's the worst speech you ever gave. What's happened to you?"

Even though I'd written the speech, I agreed with him. The fresh ideas had been excised by Bundy. *The New York Times*'s account of the speech the next day never mentioned Vietnam.

Nonetheless, Johnson was adamant about keeping Humphrey off Vietnam. Shortly after Humphrey sent the Hughes memo to Bill Moyers, news of the president's reaction bounced back: Hughes told me that Johnson was furious. He ordered an aide, "Tell Humphrey to quit sending those memos. I don't need those memos."

As Bundy pointed out, the Hughes memo was the trigger for LBJ's brutal exile of Humphrey and continuing humiliation of him over the next several years. The vice president was blocked from participating in any significant discussion of Vietnam and generally removed from anything but a ceremonial role in foreign policy. His domestic responsibilities were similarly curbed, sometimes in ways designed to demean him.

After the election, Johnson had assigned Humphrey oversight responsibilities for the space program and an aspect of the War on Poverty, part of the Great Society initiative. Not long after the Hughes memo, Joseph Califano, LBJ's special assistant for domestic policy, summoned Humphrey to his office. Humphrey went, even though Washington protocol suggested that a special assistant should go to the vice president's office for a meeting. Califano informed Humphrey that he, Califano, was taking over responsibility for space and poverty.

Despite his garrulous nature, Humphrey was normally tight-lipped about Johnson's affronts, but after the Califano humiliation, Humphrey's dismay was visible.

During the summer of 1965, Humphrey mentioned to his friend Orville Freeman, secretary of agriculture in the Johnson administration, that talk was going around that LBJ was going to send Humphrey on an overseas trip. Freeman mentioned the possibility to a reporter, and the item appeared in print. Johnson was apoplectic about leaks and canceled any plans for a trip.

Other snubs by Johnson became Washington lore. Humphrey was out on the Potomac one evening entertaining reporters on one of the two presidential yachts. Johnson happened to cruise by on the other. He had someone call over to the Humphrey boat to see who had taken it out. When Johnson heard it was Humphrey, the president established a rule that Humphrey could only use a yacht with Johnson's specific permission. The same order came down for the use of White House aircraft: LBJ had to approve.

The humiliations piled up. Humphrey hardly acknowledged what was going on—he was so nervous that word of his complaints about the president would get back to Johnson. Within the staff, we talked about it, but no one ever suggested calling a meeting with the vice president to consider how to deal with this situation. We knew the vice president would be aghast.

Why did Humphrey bring this on, speaking out, particularly given the advice he was getting from me and others? I think there are several facets to the explanation. One lies in his personal history. At the 1948 Democratic Convention, he had been warned that calling for a civil rights plank would doom his career. But he believed passionately in civil rights and delivered an electric speech in favor of the plank. In that instance, defying advice and following his conscience had turned out to be a key to ramping up his career. Humphrey may have expected to be similarly rewarded for taking a principled stand on Vietnam.

Also, he and Johnson had been colleagues for years in the Senate. Early on, Johnson had helped Humphrey settle in with some of the senators put off by the Minnesotan's brash and activist manner. Later, Johnson banked on Humphrey's liberal credentials to help remove the taint of Southern politics from his career. As the two worked together on legislation, Humphrey certainly pushed back occasionally without provoking a harsh response from Senator Johnson. Perhaps Humphrey assumed that that kind of give-and-take was still available with President Johnson.

What's more, at least at that time, Humphrey genuinely believed that escalation would be a bad mistake. Tom Hughes—whom Humphrey greatly admired—knew that escalation was imminent, and he persuaded Humphrey that the moment was passing for him to try to stop it. Humphrey went along with a last, brave effort.

On a less generous note, Humphrey always had a distressing tendency to agree with the last person to whom he spoke, and

Hughes could be brilliantly persuasive.

In any case, Humphrey's dissent produced exactly the response I'd expected from the vindictive president. Eventually, that led to the vice president's disheartening obsequiousness as the American commitment to the war expanded dramatically.

On March 8, 1965, 3,500 Marines waded onto a beach near Danang to defend an American airfield, the first American combat troops sent to Vietnam. By the end of the year, the U.S. had stationed more than 180,000 soldiers there. Three years after that first beach landing, when Johnson told the country on March 31, 1968, that he would not seek another presidential term, the troop level had reached more than half a million. By then, more than 20,000 Americans had died in the war, and hundreds of thousands of Vietnamese. American society was riven by the conflict, with regular protests in the streets and on campuses. Many traditional American allies were dismayed, and Johnson's ambitious domestic agenda had fallen by the wayside.

That leads to another question, a personal one: Why did I stay? Why continue in a role, even a marginal one, in an administration that was following a disastrous and tragic policy? As I've thought about it over the years, I've come to believe it was probably a mistake to stay. Not that my leaving would have had any impact whatsoever on Johnson's policy. But I remained part of an administration that inflicted terrible damage on Vietnam and America.

At this stage in my life, it's difficult to reconstruct all that was going through my mind more than half a century ago, but I think several factors weighed in. For one, as I mentioned, my departure wouldn't have changed anything substantive—it would have drawn at best momentary press attention, and even if I spoke out, I would have been just another dissenting voice. I also hoped I could be of service on some foreign policy issues that didn't relate to Vietnam. Humphrey had been closely involved in disarmament issues and in relations with South America and our European allies. Much work remained to be done in those areas.

More importantly, I felt intensely loyal to Hubert Humphrey. He was an honorable man, and he had been very good to me. I didn't want to abandon him at the worst time in his career.

I had a potential opportunity to leave in 1966 when Joe Slater of the Ford Foundation approached me about a job as a program officer in the Office of European and International Affairs. I was interested, and I felt obligated to tell Humphrey about the offer. He said he understood, but he urged me to stay. He insisted that my work for him remained terribly valuable. So I turned down the Ford Foundation.

Again, that was probably a mistake. I still hoped that Humphrey would be involved in vital foreign policy issues, but Vietnam was quickly overwhelming anything else on the international agenda. My influence was hugely diminished.

Several dissenters resigned from the administration around then with little or no impact on policy. My friend and colleague Jim Thomson left for Harvard and later wrote a powerful attack on the escalation in Vietnam in *The Atlantic Monthly*. George Ball left to join Lehman Brothers after losing almost every argument on Vietnam policy, though he didn't criticize the war publicly. Johnson later appointed him ambassador to the U.N.

Another friend and colleague who dissented, Tom Hughes, didn't resign and stayed on through the start of the Nixon administration. Everyone in the Johnson administration had to make the decision for himself.

The president essentially grounded Humphrey through all of 1965 and early 1966. Still, foreign policy issues would occasionally come through the office. In late 1965, for example, Vice President Humphrey received a high-level German delegation led by the cardinal archbishop of Munich. At one point, the archbishop asked Humphrey why the U.S. government discriminated against Christian trade unions in Latin America, instead favoring socialist unions. The question referred to American support for a socialist labor network that was strongly backed by the AFL-CIO. I hadn't adequately briefed Humphrey on the issue, and he responded by assuring the delegation that the U.S. government was open to working with all noncommunist labor groups. The archbishop's delegation found the answer reassuring.

This discussion took place on a Friday afternoon. When I returned to my office about 8:30 Monday morning, the vice president was already meeting with George Meaney, president of the AFL-CIO, who had insisted on seeing Humphrey before his first scheduled appointment. Humphrey later told me that Meany was furious about Humphrey's remarks to the German delegation. Humphrey should clearly understand, Meaney lectured, that in Latin America the U.S. *exclusively* supported the socialist labor network allied with the AFL.

Humphrey said that he listened to Meany's outburst but made no commitments, and the problem dissipated. But it taught me how some seemingly obscure business and political connections can have a long global reach.

The vice president and I enjoyed a more successful engagement a year later. In early 1966, a staffer for Willy Brandt, the popular mayor of Berlin, came to see me. I'd met him the year before on a trip to Germany. Brandt was running as the Social Democratic candidate for chancellor against the incumbent, Ludwig Erhard, who represented the Christian Democrats. By postwar tradition, a candidate for German chancellor would meet before the election with the American president.

President Johnson knew Brandt and liked him—like many American politicians, he had met with Brandt when he visited Berlin. But recently Brandt had made several speeches strongly critical of America's policy in Vietnam. Now, Brandt's staffer asked me: If Brandt came to Washington, would Johnson see him?

I took the question to Humphrey, who took it to Rusk. The secretary of state pointed out that it was policy for the president to see the leader of the opposition in allied countries. Nonetheless, Rusk checked with Johnson. The president said yes.

Humphrey and I knew it would be a frosty reception, so we organized an elaborate program of events—a luncheon attended by Rusk, McNamara, Senator Fulbright, and other officials; private meetings at the Pentagon and the Capitol; even an appearance on *Meet the Press*. Of course, Brandt did meet for a chilly half hour with Johnson, no photographers allowed. But the future chancellor was enormously appreciative to Humphrey and me for the success of his visit.

Humphrey's intervention for Brandt was not isolated. By that time, Humphrey had developed close relations with many Social Democratic leaders in Europe. In the early 1960s, Tage Erlander, prime minister of Sweden, would invite leading European Social Democratic leaders to spend a weekend of discussion and relaxation at his summer home in Harpsund. In July 1963, Humphrey was invited to participate. There he became friends with Brandt and another German politician, Otto Brenner, as well as with the future British prime ministers Harold Wilson and Jim Callaghan and all the Scandinavian Social Democratic leaders.

Lyndon Johnson did not like Social Democrats. Although many who visited Washington were heads of government of NATO members, it would often take a strong intervention by Humphrey to persuade Johnson to receive them.

Successes like that were rare from the vice president's position of exile.

CHAPTER 7
IN ASIA FOR LBJ

By the beginning of 1966, Elizabeth and the four kids and I were living in a two-story brick house on a corner lot on Rittenhouse Street in Chevy Chase, Maryland. The two older girls—Mary Ellen, 8, and Kathy, 6—were in elementary school. The boys—Tom, 2, and John, not yet 1—were still at home. Since Humphrey had moved to the vice presidency, my hours were better, and I could spend more time with my family. While he was in the Senate, work could drag on well into the night, and I often went into the office on weekends. Now, the days were manageable, and I rarely worked weekends.

On February 7, Humphrey was in Chicago, not expected to return until early the next morning. I was at home, but awake, when the phone rang at 11:00 p.m. It was George Ball, the deputy secretary of state, calling with a message from President Johnson that I was to deliver to Humphrey. The president had spent the last few days in Honolulu, meeting with South Vietnamese President Nguyen Van Thieu and Premier Nguyen Cao Ky along with assorted American military and security officials. The ostensible purpose was to improve coordination between the American effort in Vietnam and the South Vietnamese government, but commentators have maintained that Johnson had hastily "improvised" the conference to deflect attention from televised hearings on the war run by Senator Fulbright.

Now, Johnson had orders for Humphrey: He wanted the vice president to meet him the next day at the Los Angeles airport. After that, Humphrey and his team would begin a two-and-a-half-week, nine-destination trip to Asia with the first stop being Honolulu. In Honolulu, where the president's conference had just concluded, Humphrey was to pick up President Thieu and Premier Ky, as well as a number of top American officials, including Averell Harriman, an ambassador at large in the State Department, and McGeorge Bundy. The first stop on the trip would be Saigon. And then the president wanted Humphrey to go on to Thailand, Laos, India, Pakistan, New Zealand, Australia, the Philippines, and Korea.

Ball handed the phone to Ben Read, the executive secretary of the State Department, to relay further instructions. To meet the president in Los Angeles, Humphrey and his delegation would have to leave early the next day. Johnson had given Humphrey no advance notice, other than a vague warning to keep his schedule fluid with an admonition not to tell anyone. Humphrey hadn't even alerted Muriel. The vice president and the handful of staffers—including me—who would accompany him had had no inoculations for travel in Asia, and we'd prepared no briefing papers.

Though the White House characterized the trip as a fact-finding mission, Johnson had a promotional motive. By then, Humphrey had started making occasional positive remarks about LBJ's Vietnam policy, and the president assumed that his vice president would return with a glowing account of the progress of the war and the support for it from America's Asian allies. Then Humphrey would go on national TV and tell the American public what he had learned. Johnson hoped a report like that from his liberal vice president would bolster support for the war and, importantly, diffuse some of the criticism Johnson was taking from liberals around the country.

The outcome didn't unfold that way. The rushed diplomatic venture turned into a disaster in several respects, with some of its deepest wounds occurring after Humphrey's return to Washington.

When I got off the phone with Ben Read, I dictated a short, hasty memo for the vice president, which my wife typed up. I checked with the Secret Service, and it reported that Humphrey was scheduled to arrive home at 1:15 a.m. In those days before the official vice presidential residence was established on the grounds of the Naval Observatory, Humphrey lived in Chevy Chase, only a mile or so from my house. So at 1:15, I drove over with the news and the memo. Given Johnson's warning about keeping his schedule fluid, Humphrey wasn't entirely surprised by the assignment. But he was excited at the prospect, not least because it was a sign that he was back in the president's good graces. While Muriel slept in the bedroom, we sat down and went over plans until 2:30.

Early the next morning, Elizabeth helped me pack, I said goodbye to the kids, and I went into the office. The other Humphrey staffers on the trip would be chief of staff Bill Connell, press secretary Norman Sherman, and the vice president's secretary, Violet Williams. For more support, I called Jim Thomson, from Bundy's staff, and Carol Laise, the State Department official in charge of India and Pakistan. Fortunately, both could join on the moment's notice.

Traveling in Air Force Two, the second White House jet, we flew from Andrews Air Force Base to Los Angeles, where Humphrey met with Johnson at the airport. Afterward, with Humphrey beside him, the president read a statement on the status of the war in Vietnam. The road ahead may be long, Johnson said, but he was confident "we shall prevail" in rebuffing the aggressors and in helping to build a just society in South Vietnam.

The president emphasized the need for social reform in South Vietnam, and one purpose of Humphrey's mission was to encourage the country's leaders to improve economic and political conditions, and in particular to win support from people in the countryside. Agriculture Secretary Orville Freeman joined the trip to impart advice on agricultural issues.

From Los Angeles, we flew to Honolulu, where, after a night of rest, we picked up an assortment of travelers: Thieu; Ky; Mac Bundy; Averell Harriman; White House political aide Jack Valenti; Lloyd Hand, a Johnson pal from Texas who was chief of protocol for the State Department; and assorted staffers of American and South Vietnamese officials. A large contingent of journalists had been covering the Honolulu conference, and later, as the trip continued beyond Saigon, the reporters joined us in Air Force Two. They probably totaled 40 or 45 in all, including Tom Wicker of *The New York Times*, Phil Potter of the *Baltimore Sun*, Dick Dudman of *The St. Louis Post-Dispatch*, and a cadre of television reporters.

This was the first time I'd seen Thieu and Ky in person. Thieu was reserved and soft-spoken, but Ky—who was said by some to be the dominant force in the government— was a small, slight peacock, always turned out neatly and wearing a purple cravat. He carried a pearl-handled pistol, which he twirled around his finger on the plane, terrifying Harriman. My most vivid impression of the premier came several days later in Saigon. He accompanied our entourage while Humphrey visited an elementary school. Ky didn't bother to go in, however, and waited outside. At one point, I stepped outside myself and found Ky combing his hair and smoking a cigarette through a long cigarette holder. The expression on his face conveyed a message that thoroughly contradicted the vice president's mission: What's this guy Humphrey doing in there, wasting his time with kids? It epitomized why the South Vietnamese government was so alienated from the Vietnamese people and why officials like Ky and Thieu were so hated.

From Honolulu we flew to Guam, where we refueled and got some of our Asian inoculations, and then continued to Saigon (where we got more shots). On our first night there, current Ambassador Henry Cabot Lodge gave a dinner at his residence for the Humphrey delegation and for the South Vietnamese officials. One of the first courses was shark fin soup, a Vietnamese delicacy. Lodge got violently sick from it and disappeared for the next day. (Someone had warned me it could be dangerous for the uninitiated, and I only tasted it.)

We were in Saigon for just over two days. Humphrey met with Thieu and Ky, as well as General William Westmoreland, who headed the U.S. military operation, and various other U.S. and South Vietnamese officers and officials. The briefings for the most part were extremely optimistic: The war was going well; the South Vietnamese army was becoming more reliable; the South Vietnamese people were behind their government. At one point, Humphrey took Jim Thomson and me aside. We were welcome to sit in on his meetings, Humphrey said, but we would be much more valuable to him if we ventured out to talk to people on our own. He pointed out correctly that the officials he met were unlikely to say anything critical of the American effort; people would tell us things that they wouldn't tell him.

So I met with Phil Habib, the political counselor on the U.S. embassy staff, a very savvy career Foreign Service officer. The two of us had a long lunch in his house. Without being disloyal to Ambassador Lodge or the president, he conveyed his skepticism about Johnson's policy in Vietnam. Contrary to what Thieu, Ky, and the American military leaders were telling Humphrey and what McNamara was telling Johnson, things were going badly. We were not winning the war or the "hearts and minds" of the people. (Two years later, Habib—then deputy assistant secretary of state—gave a briefing at the Pentagon that's widely regarded as turning around U.S. officials and eventually Johnson himself on the idea that the American military could beat back the Viet Cong and defeat North Vietnam.)

Jim Thomson found his own skeptical sources. By then, Ed Lansdale had been sent to Vietnam to try to enhance the "pacification" program, the plan to win loyalty from rural Vietnamese. One member of Lansdale's small team was a Thomson friend, Daniel Ellsberg, who five years later would release the Pentagon Papers. Thomson met with Lansdale and Ellsberg and heard another pessimistic assessment of the situation.

Later, I visited the countryside by helicopter. One of my Chevy Chase neighbors was a top official in the CIA who had been dispatched to Vietnam. When he saw my name on the manifest of visitors, he got in touch and asked if I'd like to get outside Saigon to observe what was going on. Through his arrangements, I had encounters with American and South Vietnamese officers and some CIA officials. None were immediately under the thumb of the leaders in Saigon, and their comments were far more pessimistic than the official line. I let Humphrey know what I had learned, and later, toward the end of the trip when we prepared a report for President Johnson, I urged that we reflect some of the pessimism.

Humphrey had decided he would make his lone public statement at the end of the Saigon visit, and Thomson and I wrote up a rough draft—an essentially bland commentary that talked about the American commitment and again emphasized the need for social reforms. Somehow, a copy of the draft ended up in the hands of Harriman, who accosted me furiously. He was known as "The Crocodile" because of his habit of snapping at people. He grabbed me by the front of my shirt collar as if he were going to strangle me. "John, John, did you write this?" he demanded. "This is terrible. This is the worst statement I've ever seen. If Humphrey issues this, I'll resign."

I assured him the document was nothing more than preliminary notes. We were still working on it. What's more, Humphrey had insisted that when we had a final draft, we should run it past him—Harriman—before releasing it.

That calmed down The Crocodile. He and I were essentially allies on this trip, and our views on Vietnam were similar. To this day, I'm not sure what angered him about the draft. I suspect he somehow thought we were trying to circumvent him and release the statement without his approval. In any case, the rewritten and Harriman-approved release went out and drew little attention, though Tom Wicker of the *Times*, among others, worried in a column that the vice president was overly optimistic about the possibility of success. We learned later that Humphrey had also cleared the statement with Jack Valenti, who had been assigned by LBJ to keep an eye on the vice president's activities. Valenti would send a cable to the White House every morning.

Mac Bundy and a few other officials flew home from Saigon, but Harriman stayed with us, along with the large press contingent. From Saigon, we flew to Bangkok, Thailand, where Humphrey assured the anxious Thai leaders, including Prime Minister Thanom Kittikachorn, of the American commitment to defending South Vietnam. The Thais had allowed the United States to use Thai air bases for bombing raids on North Vietnam, and the Thai leadership worried about threats from the North Vietnamese and China. The Humphrey delegation stayed in a series of guesthouses that belonged to the king of Thailand, and at a dinner one night, the king gave gifts of silver—mine was a cigarette box—to everyone in the delegation.

The next day, a Monday, we made a one-day trip to Laos, a stop that led to the first of several unfortunate blunders by Humphrey during the trip. Under an agreement that Averell Harriman helped draw up in 1962, Laos was considered a neutral country among the competing interests of the United States, the Soviet Union, China, and North Vietnam. The shaky Laotian coalition government was led by Premier Souvanna Phouma.

Our visit started with a meeting with Laotian officials, and then a lunch hosted by the premier. In remarks at the lunch, Souvanna Phouma acknowledged that the U.S. was providing considerable aid to his country, but he said Laos needed more, that his people were leading a spartan life. In particular, he said, Laos needed hard currency. Meantime, we were served a lavish lunch, the most elaborate of the trip. It started with French champagne, followed by Norwegian salmon, pheasant from Australia, an Indonesian vegetable, French wine, a fancy fruit from another Asian country, and then French cognac with coffee. Afterward, Humphrey mentioned to several of us that for all the talk of the need for hard currency, there wasn't a thing served at lunch that came from Laos.

Following the lunch, Humphrey, Harriman, Souvanna, and I moved to the premier's study for more talk. Souvanna said he understood that things were going badly in Vietnam for the Americans, and he suggested to Humphrey and Harriman that if it became necessary, the U.S. should not hesitate to use nuclear weapons. Both the Americans were startled at the suggestion and ignored it. Later on the trip, Humphrey said something to a journalist that led him to figure out that Souvanna had raised the nuclear option, and a story appeared with that report. The story deeply embarrassed the premier, who was supposed to be a neutralist in the region.

After the luxurious lunch in Laos, we flew back to Thailand, where we were entertained at another long, elaborate, wine-filled banquet, which I think contributed to another Humphrey blunder. The United States was already giving massive aid to Thailand, but because the Thais allowed U.S. bombing flights from Thai soil, the country had considerable leverage; the Thais kept asking for more aid. The American ambassador in Bangkok, a Foreign Service officer named Graham Martin, was deeply sympathetic to the Thai leaders and always recommended honoring the requests. Secretary of State Dean Rusk kept turning them down. Martin didn't relent and continued to lobby for more aid.

When the long, soggy Thai banquet finally ended, Humphrey rode with Martin in the ambassador's limousine back to the residence where the vice president was staying. In the car, Martin pulled out a communique and asked Humphrey to sign it. By then, Humphrey was weary from enduring several nights with limited sleep and a long day with complicated meetings and two huge feasts. He normally drank little, but drinking was hard to avoid at these ceremonial meals, and he'd downed several glasses of wine. He glanced at the document Martin handed him, but he assumed it was routine, a formal goodbye of some sort. So he signed it.

Throughout the trip, I was in the habit of stopping in at the vice president's room at the end of the day to go over plans for the next day and to brief him on what was to be expected. Something must have troubled him about Martin's document, because when I arrived at his room that night, he asked, "John, what did you think of that communique?"

This was the first I'd heard of it. "What communique?"

"You didn't see the document Ambassador Martin had me sign?"

"I didn't see anything."

"Oh, fine. Forget about it. Not important."

But it was important. Martin had played a trick. The document Humphrey had signed was a promise by the U.S. government to provide substantial additional aid to Thailand. Now the promise was backed by the signature of the vice president.

The news broke almost immediately. Tom Wicker of *The New York Times* had a stringer in Bangkok who somehow got his hands on the communique. At 2:30 in the morning, he took it to Wicker's hotel room. Wicker immediately recognized the importance of the document and filed a story, scooping the dozens of other reporters on the trip.

When I got to the airport in the morning for the next leg of the journey, I saw Phil Potter of the *Baltimore Sun*, in many ways the dean of Asian correspondents, berating Humphrey's press man, Norman Sherman. Potter was six-foot-three or so, and Sherman was probably a foot shorter. Potter had Sherman by the shirt collar, screaming, "You goddamn whores for *The New York Times*!" He thought Sherman had leaked the communique to the *Times*, which of course wasn't what had happened. It took considerable powers of persuasion to calm Potter down. And the unfortunate echoes of that communique would come back to bedevil Humphrey.

Our next stop was Pakistan, then led by Ayub Khan. American-Pakistani relations had soured recently, and aid to Pakistan and India had been suspended, ostensibly because the two countries were fighting over Kashmir. At the same time, the Johnson administration thought Pakistan and India didn't take seriously enough the threat to the region by the Chinese. After a discussion with Khan, Humphrey let him know that $50 million in American aid would be forthcoming.

The most notable event on the Pakistan stop came by way of foreign minister Zulfikar Ali Bhutto, a hard-drinking, Oxford-educated playboy (and the father of Benazir Bhutto, who, like her father, later became prime minister of Pakistan). Bhutto was a skilled diplomat, but on our visit, his coup was to throw a party for the press corps—only the press corps. By all reports, it was a terrific event—the reporters loved it, and they alone attended.

In India, Humphrey had a specific message from Johnson to convey to the new prime minister, Indira Gandhi: Aid would only be forthcoming if India used it to advance agricultural progress by such actions as creating a land grant system or building fertilizer plants.

For some reason, Johnson didn't like Indians, and he believed the Kennedy administration had been persuaded by Ambassador John Kenneth Galbraith to allocate far too much aid to India. The Indians directed much of the aid, Soviet style, to building steel mills and other heavy industries; meantime, the country was spending billions importing food for its large population. American aid should go toward improving agricultural productivity, Humphrey told Mrs. Gandhi.

The Indians got the message. Within three years, with the arrival of the "Green Revolution," India was self-sufficient in food production, and within five years it was exporting substantial quantities of food. That was easily the most useful development that came out of the trip. After India, things went downhill again.

The flight from India to Australia took 14 hours. During the flight, Bill Connell told me the delegation should meet that night to get started on the trip report, which we would need to deliver to President Johnson soon after our return. I told Connell that was a terrible idea—everyone was tired already, and Humphrey and Harriman were scheduled to have dinner with Robert Menzies, who had just resigned as Australian prime minister. That dinner will run late, I said, and we'll need to wait for Humphrey and Harriman to join us, so we wouldn't even be able to start the meeting until 10:00 p.m. or so. But Connell prevailed.

Harriman and Menzies were old friends. Both had spent important time in London, and both were friends of Winston Churchill. With reminiscences and wine, the congenial dinner dragged on, and it was after 11:00 p.m. before the delegation could gather to discuss the tenor of the report to Johnson. Humphrey was weary, as was almost everyone else.

At some point during the discussion, Jack Valenti repeated a common bromide of the time—if we don't stop the communists in Vietnam, within a few years they'll be in Honolulu, then San Francisco. A few minutes later, someone else repeated the comment. Eventually, Humphrey picked it up too, and he remarked that what Jack said was true—if we don't stop them now, they'll be in Honolulu, then San Francisco.

This was too much for Jim Thomson. He knew Asia. He'd grown up part of the time in China with missionary parents. He spoke fluent Chinese. He'd been a Vietnam expert for Bill Bundy in the State Department and now for Mac Bundy and the NSC staff. Quietly, Thomson had been a vigorous opponent of Johnson's Vietnam strategy. So Thomson challenged Humphrey directly in front of the entire delegation. He went on for two or three minutes before Averell Harriman suddenly stood up and announced, "Ladies and gentlemen, I think it's time for all of us to go to bed. This meeting is over."

Humphrey was furious. Thomson had embarrassed the vice president of the United States in front of 16 or 18 people. Almost immediately, Thomson realized he'd made a mistake and wrote a letter of apology to Humphrey, which he had delivered the next morning. But Humphrey remained angry—and later, in front of Harriman and me, he lit into Thomson, petulantly charging that Thomson had no respect for him and claiming he didn't need Thomson's advice. It was a sad display, and I'd almost never seen Humphrey go off like that.

The morning after that first confrontation, Humphrey conferred with Australia's new prime minister, Harold Holt, by far the most enthusiastic supporter of LBJ's policy among Asian leaders. Australia had already sent a 1,200-man fighting force to Vietnam. After that meeting, Holt held a luncheon for Humphrey with 200 or so members of Parliament and other Australian notables. On his way to the banquet hall, Humphrey had to pass a noisy contingent of demonstrators protesting American policy in Vietnam and singling him out. One called Humphrey "the world's No. 1 warmonger." Another held a sign that read, "Hitler Himmler Humphrey." The vice president tried to shrug the protests off.

At the luncheon, Holt gave Humphrey a long, glowing introduction and assured the vice president of Australia's solid support for the war in Vietnam. What's more, whether knowingly or not, Holt echoed Jack Valenti's Munich-tinged point that if we don't stop the communists now, they will just keep going.

Jim Thomson and I had written a speech for Humphrey, a moderate, noncommittal statement that praised the Australians for their friendship and loyalty. But Humphrey—always easily influenced by his environment—got worked up by Holt's introduction and never glanced at the prepared speech. Instead, he delivered a virtual rant—proclaiming America's determination to win the war and going on with the idea that China was behind the unrest in Vietnam and elsewhere in Asia. As Tom Wicker reported, "He said Peking was testing the theory of wars of national liberation in the 'test tube of Vietnam' and he called the war there a 'pilot project of Communist strategy.'" And Humphrey raised again the specter of fighting communists on America's own shores if the enemy weren't stopped now in Vietnam.

Harriman and I attended the luncheon, and afterward The Crocodile again accosted me in fury. "John, did you write that speech? That's the worst speech I ever heard! If Humphrey ever gives that speech again, I'll resign!" Of course, I assured him that the prepared speech was far different and that I agreed Humphrey's comments were way off base. Harriman cooled down, and we were friends once more.

Holt and his supporters responded enthusiastically to Humphrey's comments, but for Harriman, me, and other skeptics of Johnson's policy, the direction of Humphrey's comments was deeply troubling. It was clear the vice president was growing increasingly hawkish as the trip progressed, particularly on the idea of Chinese expansion. He seemed to have forgotten the point that Tom Hughes and I had raised about the indigenous nature of the conflict in Vietnam. Several times I broached my concerns with him. But he did not want to be confronted on it. He was very aware that Johnson loyalists Jack Valenti and Lloyd Hand were on the plane.

That afternoon, we flew to New Zealand, where we were greeted by a fierce rainstorm and an agitated crowd of damp protesters. At a news conference in Wellington with Prime Minister Keith Holyoake, Humphrey made another remark that reverberated at home. Bobby Kennedy was building an increasingly high profile as an opponent of Johnson's Vietnam policy, and he had called for bringing the Viet

Cong into a coalition government in South Vietnam. At the Wellington press conference, a reporter asked Humphrey what he thought of Kennedy's proposal. The vice president was grandly dismissive, saying that communists had a history of subverting democratic government from within. Allowing the Viet Cong to join in governing would be like "putting a fox in the chicken coop; soon there wouldn't be any chickens left." Newspapers around the world picked up the story. The fact that Kennedy and Humphrey were already talked of as future presidential rivals only amplified the remark.

The next stop on the wearying journey was an 11-hour flight to Manila, the Philippines, where a large crowd of anti-war demonstrators protested in front of the American embassy. Humphrey conferred with the new president, Ferdinand Marcos, and we met with Bill Blair, who had left the ambassadorship of Denmark to become the ambassador here. Both Humphrey and I knew Blair, and he felt free to speak frankly. He was despondent about the state of the Philippines and scathing about Marcos, whom he thought was incompetent and corrupt. Blair was even more severe about Marcos's wife, Imelda. Blair hated her and thought she brought out the worst instincts in her husband.

The final stop on the tour was Seoul, South Korea. Fortunately, little of import happened there, perhaps because we were all exhausted by nearly two weeks of hectic travel. Humphrey wanted to stop and rest in Hong Kong for a day, but Valenti checked with the White House. LBJ ordered us to come straight back.

During the long flight home, we worked on the report about the trip, which the vice president would deliver to Johnson. The discussion was contentious. On the one hand, Bill Connell and Jack Valenti wanted an upbeat assessment. Valenti was a gentleman about it, but he kept repeating, "The president wants optimism, the president wants optimism!" On the other, Harriman, Thomson, Norman Sherman, and I wanted to emphasize the limits of what was being achieved in Vietnam. Except for the leaders in South Vietnam, Thailand, and Australia, virtually all the top government officials in Asia were critical or at least skeptical of American policy, though none would express their concerns publicly for fear of alienating Johnson. For the most part, Humphrey stayed aloof from the bitter arguments on the plane, though he was shown in a wire photograph looking over a draft of the report with Harriman and me. We were still working on the document when the plane landed at Andrews Air Force Base in Maryland, after 15 hours in the air.

A helicopter whisked the delegation to the South Lawn of the White House, which had been flooded by lights so the television news cameras could record the landing. Johnson greeted Humphrey with a hug, and he shook hands with the delegation. The welcoming party included Dean Rusk, Mac Bundy, even the president's daughter Luci and the family's dogs. In a prepared statement released earlier, Humphrey said, "I return, Mr. President, with a deep sense of confidence in our cause—and its ultimate triumph."

Elizabeth and the kids met me at the White House and took me home. I was thrilled to see them but exhausted, and I still had to finish the report.

The next day, Humphrey gave a briefing to congressional leaders and top administration officials in the Cabinet Room at the White House. I attended too. Johnson himself dominated the meeting, but Humphrey repeated that he saw promise in the progress of the war. Significantly, only two old Humphrey antagonists, Southern Bloc members Richard Russell and Strom Thurmond, spoke up in praise of the trip. Humphrey went on to several other congressional meetings without Johnson present, and the exchanges were more open.

When I got away, I pulled in Ted Van Dyk, Humphrey's director of communications and a skilled editor, to help me complete the report. Van Dyk shared my views on Vietnam, but Connell—still lobbying heavily for optimism—kept his eye on what we were doing.

Van Dyk and I spent two days on the draft, finally finishing at 3:00 one morning. We ordered up a White House car to take the document directly to Humphrey's house in Chevy Chase so Connell couldn't get his hands on it. I went home and went to bed. At 8:30 the next morning I got a frantic call from Connell: Where's that report? I told him it was already in Humphrey's hands.

The report Van Dyk and I forwarded was a compromise assessment, around 35 pages long. We tried to tone down the optimism without giving full throat to the concerns many of us shared. We did not take on the question of sending more troops. Humphrey thanked us for our efforts without making any specific comments. He sat on the report for a day or so, then sent it to the White House. Silence ensued. Johnson had been hoping for a robust endorsement of his policy, and this fell well short. White House officials shaved it drastically to around seven pages and released it a few days later to almost no attention. As Humphrey put it in his 1976 memoir, *The Education of a Public Man*, "We had labored hard and brought forth a mouse."[8]

That put an official end to the Asian tour, but the repercussions continued.

A week or so after we returned, Humphrey appeared before an informal group of senators in Mike Mansfield's office to discuss what he'd learned. Protocol prevented a vice president from appearing before the Senate Foreign Relations Committee, so Mansfield invited a handful of committee members to discuss the trip with Humphrey. I accompanied the vice president. Most of those gathered were Humphrey friends—including William Fulbright, Frank Church, Wayne Morse, Gene McCarthy, and Mansfield himself. Humphrey assumed he was among allies, but the questioning turned hostile. Fulbright zeroed in on the Thai communique that Humphrey had mistakenly signed. At one point, the senator asked whether Humphrey thought President Johnson was trying to build a Great Society in Asia. Humphrey—not using his best judgment—said, yes, that's probably right. Someone else asked if the commitment Johnson was making to Asia was tantamount to the Marshall Plan commitment to Europe after World War II. Again, Humphrey, not being careful, said that was probably right.

Fulbright argued angrily that the Johnson administration was expanding the Vietnam venture far beyond what Congress had authorized. He was probably still smarting over his support of the Tonkin Gulf Resolution two years before and saw this as an opportunity for Congress to regain ground. He leaked Humphrey's comments to Phil Geyelin, then of *The Wall Street Journal*, who wrote a critical column. Days later, Eric Sevareid of CBS News, a longtime friend of Humphrey's, grilled the vice president on the same point.

Dean Rusk never provided the additional aid to Thailand, but the entire incident was an embarrassment for Humphrey, as he acknowledged privately to me, and it contributed to the generally

---

8 Humphrey, Hubert H., *The Education of a Public Man*, Doubleday (1976), p. 337.

bad press Humphrey was getting over the trip. Johnson saw the way the media was reacting and dropped further mention of his vice president's excursion.

But for Humphrey, the trip led to a dramatic pivot. Just a year before, he'd spoken up at a National Security Council meeting against expanding the war. While exiled by Johnson, he'd stayed largely silent on Vietnam, and even during the Asian trip, he spoke in generalities about progress and about the threat of communist expansion. His rant at the Australian dinner was as outspoken as he got. But within weeks of returning from Asia, he began to speak out in favor of Johnson's escalation of the war. Indeed, over the next year and a half, he became the administration's most vocal salesman of a strong American military effort, outselling even Johnson himself. What's more, where he had formerly held a nuanced view of the communist threat, he now assailed China as a predatory force in Asia, working to spread revolution in countries well beyond Vietnam. As Arthur Schlesinger reportedly told him in a later meeting, Humphrey was still laboring under the outdated idea that communism was a monolithic force internationally.

The new, hawkish stance alienated his longtime liberal allies and, worse, destroyed his credibility with the public. What was going through his mind? Why the change of view?

In his 1976 memoir, Humphrey offered several explanations, none particularly convincing. First, he said the official briefings in Vietnam didn't play as much of a factor as did his conversations with Asian leaders, who highlighted the need to halt communist expansion. More importantly, he was moved by the courage and determination of the American troops, who thought they were fighting for a just cause. In the book, he went on to blame the isolation of the White House, where information was funneled through a handful of trusted advisers. He suggested that he might have held to his more skeptical views about aggressive military action had he remained in the Senate, where he would have had wider sources of information.[9]

But, of course, as vice president, Humphrey was bombarded with dissenting views—from his staff, colleagues, friends, reporters. Skeptical opinions about the war were everywhere in the air. Humphrey chose not to accept them.

---

9 *The Education of a Public Man*, p. 337, pp. 350-351.

I can suggest a number of reasons why. Certainly, the most obvious was that he was eager to be received back in the embrace of President Johnson. LBJ had thrown his arms around Humphrey when he stepped off the helicopter on the South Lawn—a striking metaphor for the place Humphrey wanted to be. The center of power sings a siren song to many people, one that can bend logic and beliefs. After the Asian trip, for example, Averell Harriman made several public statements condemning those who dissented on American efforts in Vietnam. He was a steadfast skeptic of the U.S. strategy, but he spoke out against others voicing similar concerns, arguing that it gave encouragement to the enemy. Why? Harriman was addicted to staying close to power, and he desperately wanted to retain access to the White House.

Humphrey had been seriously wounded by his banishment, and the chance to return to the White House no doubt colored his attitude and may have affected his thinking. In Vietnam, he got an earful of promising news and statistics from General Westmoreland, Ambassador Lodge, and other American officials, as well as from President Thieu and Premier Ky. Though the vice president heard some dissent from Harriman, Thomson, and me, the steady diet of optimistic evaluations made it easy to ignore the pessimists.

The noisy and increasingly personal attacks on Johnson and Humphrey himself probably also weighed on Humphrey's attitude. Some of them—comparing the vice president to Hitler, for example—were patently unfair. And the relentless criticism from longtime friends pained Humphrey, as those close to him could readily see. The confrontation with Fulbright shortly after the return was particularly wounding. It's natural for a man under fire to assume a defensive crouch, and that sense of being assailed may have pushed Humphrey to go overboard in promoting Johnson's strategy in Vietnam.

All these factors likely worked together to twist Humphrey into a stance that contradicted his earlier beliefs and pushed him to advocate a disastrous policy. For more than two years he stayed with it.

CHAPTER 8
CHEERLEADER FOR THE WAR

As Humphrey continued to speak out on behalf of President Johnson's Vietnam policy throughout 1966 and 1967, I kept closely posted on the status of the war through Tom Hughes, author of the 1966 memo that led to Humphrey's exile. About once a month, I would walk over to his office in the State Department, and for an hour or so we would talk about what was happening in Vietnam. By then, Hughes had been elevated to director of the Bureau of Intelligence and Research (INR), and he oversaw several hundred analysts and researchers and had access to raw intelligence from a portfolio of American agencies, from the CIA to the National Security Agency to the intelligence units run by the Army, Navy, and Air Force. Hughes would regularly produce an assessment that would be passed to his boss, Dean Rusk, and beyond.

Hughes's mandate was to deliver intelligence, not policy recommendations, and by his account he held to that standard, though his analysis of the situation was usually realistic, far from the optimism the administration wanted. A 1969 assessment of the INR's role (only released in 2004) documents the agency's record of dissent on Vietnam and Hughes's strong leadership.[10]

With me, he was candid. He was a soft-spoken, dignified Midwesterner, and he and I agreed that the war was a terrible mistake. Dean Rusk knew how Hughes felt, but he kept him in the job because he honored the independence of the INR, and he trusted Hughes.

I also kept abreast of what was going on in Vietnam and the government through private conversations with an assortment of journalists. I am an unabashed supporter of the press and have almost always been impressed by the journalists I encountered. Many became friends. With rare exceptions, the journalists I knew were intelligent and committed to meeting the public's need to know. While journalism is as fiercely competitive as politics, I've always preferred the company of journalists to politicians.

One of my most enjoyable experiences involving the press was the pair of meetings I had during the summer of 1964 with Walter Lippmann, then at the height of his fame as America's most influential columnist. His assistant, Elizabeth Midgley, who did research for his column, was responsible for introducing Lippmann to bright young men and women who could keep him abreast of the views of the next generation. As her friend, I readily accepted her offer to introduce me to Lippmann.

We met twice in the book-lined study of his stately home next door to the Washington Cathedral several months before President Johnson would choose his vice presidential running mate. Although Lippmann was already a sharp critic of U.S. policy in Vietnam, we did not discuss the war. His questioning focused primarily on Senator Humphrey's qualifications to serve as a future president. Although Lippmann did not know Humphrey well, he eventually gave him a timely endorsement for vice president. Later, he invited my wife and me to attend his annual garden party, one of the highlights of the Washington spring social season.

Many of the journalists with whom I talked could be impressively knowledgeable about Vietnam, and sometimes they had access to administration sources who were unavailable to me. Some of my regular acquaintances included Max Frankel and Tad Szulc of *The*

---

10 The 1969 assessment and a retrospective introduction by Tom Hughes are contained in the National Security Archive, a repository of information run independently; the INR material is listed under "Intelligence and Vietnam: The Top Secret 1969 State Department Study."

New York Times, Dick Dudman of the *St. Louis Post-Dispatch*, Chalmers Roberts of *The Washington Post*, and Peter Lisagor of the *Chicago Daily News*.

One of my best sources was Henry Brandon, the Washington correspondent of the British paper *The Sunday Times*. He'd been in Washington for years and enjoyed a large circle of well-connected friends, from Henry Kissinger to John Kennedy to Kay Graham, the publisher of *The Washington Post*. I met him during the 1964 campaign when he happened to sit beside me on the press bus. We started talking, and he was impressed by my knowledge of arms control issues. He had a private house and a chef, and after we met, he would invite me to lunch for forthright conversations.

Brandon had access to the top people in the Johnson administration. He could phone Robert McNamara, for example, and the secretary of defense would take the call. I learned more from him than he ever learned from me—which was the case with many of my journalist acquaintances.

Lyndon Johnson, of course, was paranoid about leaks, and he knew Humphrey liked reporters and talked too much. The vice president assumed he was being wiretapped, and, as top staff, we had the same concern about our phones. Someone told me once that a White House insider had complained that I was talking to too many journalists. No one ever chided me about it, however, and I was certainly careful. I might make an appointment over the office phone to see a reporter, but I would almost never speak about anything substantive. Instead, we would meet outside the office. Even then, I was careful not to reveal too much, and nothing that might embarrass the vice president.

Yet it was hard not to run afoul of the increasingly paranoid Johnson administration. In late 1966, I stopped for a few days in Madrid at the end of an extended European trip during which I'd been talking to an array of government officials and others. While in Madrid, I stayed at the apartment of my friend Tad Szulc, the *Times* correspondent stationed there. In those days, *Times* foreign correspondents lived in grand style, and Szulc's apartment was big and comfortable. What's more, Szulc was well connected with Spanish officialdom—in some respects, better connected than the American ambassador. For example, for days I tried unsuccessfully through the embassy to get appointments with several ranking Spanish ministers. Finally, Szulc made two calls, and I landed the interviews.

When I got back to Washington, I wrote up a report for Humphrey, which he circulated. Not long after, as Humphrey later recounted to me, he was at a State Department reception, and Dean Rusk called him aside. Rusk told Humphrey that I'd written a good memo, but I'd made a mistake in Madrid—I'd stayed with the *Times* reporter. Rusk pointed toward the White House. That wouldn't go well over there, he said. Apparently, the embassy had alerted Rusk to my lodging.

As it turned out, the Johnson administration wasn't the only government keeping an eye on me. Twice while I worked for Humphrey, I suspect I was approached by the Soviet KGB. One incident was confirmed. Eugene Foley, the head of the Small Business Administration and a warm Humphrey backer, had a wide circle of acquaintances, one of whom was an official of the Soviet embassy in Washington. One time, not long after the 1964 election, Foley asked me if I'd have lunch with his friend. I readily agreed, and the embassy official and I had a pleasant lunch. He asked lots of questions, and I was appropriately discreet. At the time, neither Foley nor I had any idea the man was KGB. But the FBI was tapping the man's phone and alerted the White House to my lunch. Fortunately, nothing ever came of it.

The second incident was more ambiguous. I had a Polish friend whose wife worked for the United Nations, and they were living in Vienna. On a trip to Europe, I visited Vienna, and my friend and his wife invited me to join them at a Viennese ball. Their neighbors, a young Austrian couple, also sat at our table. The neighbor's wife was quite attractive, and she took what seemed to be an unusual interest in me. She asked me to dance several times and later invited me to lunch.

At the lunch, she asked a number of piercing questions about my work, and I got suspicious. She wanted to have another lunch or dinner, but I begged off. Vienna was a hotbed of intrigue in those days, and I suspect she was an agent trying to glean whatever information she could.

With Humphrey back in the good graces of President Johnson, his schedule turned more hectic, and I saw him less. Occasionally I would arrange small dinners for him with experts in areas of foreign policy, usually academics. I stayed away from Vietnam, but instead focused on issues around the globe. We'd meet in a private dining room in a restaurant or perhaps at the Cosmos Club. It was usually just the expert, Humphrey, and me, but sometimes another staffer would come along, and occasionally Tom Hughes would join us.

For example, to buff Humphrey's knowledge of the Soviet Union's role in the world, I arranged a dinner with Zbigniew Brzezinski, who had been briefly at the State Department but was then back at Columbia University. In those days, Brzezinski was a fierce cold warrior who took a hard line on the Soviets. To counteract his views, I set up a second dinner with Marshall Shulman, another Soviet expert also at Columbia, who favored a less confrontational approach to the communists. Humphrey thoughtfully absorbed the opinions of both, but his tilt was clearly toward Shulman.

As the American troop buildup and bombing accelerated in Vietnam, Humphrey's comments about the war became more strident. In part that was because he became the chief cheerleader for Democratic candidates in the midterm elections, and he and Johnson wanted to support candidates who backed an aggressive Vietnam policy. Humphrey rarely talked to me about politics, but several biographers suggest that after the Asia trip, Humphrey allowed his dream of one day being president to blossom again. He believed that his path to the White House depended on the successful prosecution of the war. As it turned out, the 1966 election results didn't deliver a clear verdict on the war; the Republicans made gains in both the House and Senate, but the Democrats retained control of both houses.

Though Humphrey went around the country making strong speeches in support of Johnson's aggressive war policy, he never asked me to write the speeches—he knew where I stood. Instead, he had a standard address that he would tune to the audience he faced. And, as usual, he ventured at length well beyond the text.

He was more adventurous than Johnson in speaking before potentially hostile groups—by then, the president was largely limiting himself to appearing before military audiences. Humphrey increasingly had to confront noisy protestors. In February 1967, for example, he ventured to Stanford University, addressing a large gathering of students and faculty. He told them, among other things, that if John Kennedy were still president, he would be pursuing the same Vietnam policy that President Johnson was pursuing. Though some people applauded his comments, he was heckled, and several hundred students and faculty walked out. Afterward, his car was swarmed by students in a surly confrontation that was widely condemned by the commentators in the media.

By then, Bobby Kennedy was emerging as the most prominent politician dissenting on Johnson's Vietnam policy, and reporters often referenced Kennedy and Humphrey as potential presidential rivals. Though Humphrey had eventually gotten along well with John Kennedy, he never forgave Bobby for promoting the false claim that he had been a slacker in World War II, a story that surfaced in the 1960 West Virginia primary. It surely galled Humphrey to see Bobby now embraced by the liberals who were Humphrey's friends and had once been his strong supporters.

Those friends never stopped trying to persuade Humphrey to change his views on Vietnam. In the summer of 1966, for example, Allard Lowenstein, the anti-war activist and later congressman who had briefly been a foreign policy aide to Humphrey in late 1959, arranged to visit Humphrey in his office with some like-minded colleagues.

Humphrey wasn't moved, and, for his part, the vice president kept trying to win the liberals over. In the spring of 1967, at Humphrey's urging, a handful of his liberal colleagues gathered for a private dinner with him at Joseph Rauh's house in Washington to discuss Vietnam. The group had the imprimatur of Americans for Democratic Action and included ADA founder Arthur Schlesinger, new ADA president John Kenneth Galbraith, and past president Joe Rauh. Humphrey himself had been an ADA president in 1949–50. Albert Eisele provides a close account of the gathering in his book *Almost to the Presidency*.[11] After pleasantries, the discussion grew heated, with Schlesinger turning strongly critical, particularly asserting that Humphrey's belief in a globally monolithic communist threat was outdated. At the end of the evening, Humphrey and Schlesinger embraced, but neither side moved the other to change its views. By that point, Humphrey was used to criticism, even from old friends, but I recall that he was shaken by the evening at Rauh's.

Yet Humphrey continued to speak out strongly in favor of the war, despite increasingly personal criticism from his old liberal allies. What's more, he railed against the anti-war activists whose protests

---

11 Eisele, Albert, *Almost to the Presidency*, Piper Publications (1972), pp. 252-255.

were becoming noisier and attention-grabbing.

President Johnson continued to dispatch his vice president on trips around the world. In March 1967, Humphrey visited seven countries in Europe, with the underlying mission to explain and perhaps win over skeptical allies about the military buildup in Vietnam. By press accounts, he served as a good ambassador, but he didn't win over any skeptics. I didn't go to Europe with him, but in October that year, I joined Humphrey as he visited Saigon again, this time to witness the inauguration of President Thieu. Thieu and Ky had taken power in a 1965 military coup, but now they were wrapping themselves in the trappings of democracy after being endorsed in a sketchy election. We were joined by a smaller press contingent than during our last Saigon trip, but that was the first time I met Johnny Apple of *The New York Times*, who was just finishing up his stint as a Saigon correspondent. He would become a lifelong friend.

The trip continued to Malaysia and Indonesia, but it resulted in little of substance, and Humphrey avoided the gaffes that had haunted his previous Asia tour. A few weeks after he returned, he left on a nine-nation goodwill tour of Africa. Again, little of substance came from the trip.

Throughout the two years after the first Asian tour, I occasionally took foreign trips myself with Humphrey's encouragement. Several times I visited European allies. And in Washington, I received frequent visits from foreign officials, many of them acquaintances from the days when the Alliance for Progress thrived. In almost all these exchanges, we tried to stay away from discussions of Vietnam.

On March 31, 1968, I flew with Humphrey and a delegation to Mexico City, where the vice president was to sign an agreement attaching the United States to an arms-control treaty that would make 21 Latin American nations a nuclear-free zone. As it turned out, President Johnson had scheduled a major public address for that evening. The president was enduring a bruising few months. After McNamara had either resigned or been pushed out—accounts differ—Johnson had appointed the longtime Washington insider Clark Clifford as secretary of defense. By then, more than half a million American soldiers were in Vietnam, yet the Viet Cong and North Vietnamese troops had launched the so-called Tet Offensive that attacked American and South Vietnamese strongholds throughout South Vietnam. Though the offensive has come to be seen as a military failure, at that time its surprise and impact were treated as a devastating setback by many Americans.

Meantime, opposition to the war was building steadily in the United States. On March 12, Senator Gene McCarthy, an outspoken critic, almost defeated President Johnson in that year's first presidential primary in New Hampshire. Days later, Bobby Kennedy announced that he was running for president. And Clifford, the new secretary of defense, had assembled a panel of elder statesmen, including Dean Acheson and Harriman, who counseled Johnson against continuing the war.

As the hour of Johnson's speech approached, Humphrey and the delegation and a pack of reporters gathered at the Mexico City residence of Ambassador Tony Freeman for a formal dinner with the Mexican leaders. Before it began, several of us, including Humphrey, Muriel Humphrey, Freeman, and Mexican President Gustavo Diaz Ordaz, settled into the ambassador's study to watch the speech on television. Other members of the delegation and several journalists listened over a scratchy radio in the ambassador's library. Johnson's announcement of a substantial reduction in bombing raids and a renewed push for negotiations led by Averell Harriman sounded promising. Then we listened in stunned silence as Johnson declared that he would not run for another term.

Almost immediately, reporters outside the ambassador's study and others outside the residence clamored to question Humphrey. When he emerged after 20 minutes or so, he acknowledged that Johnson had warned him that he might announce his withdrawal from the campaign—a secret the garrulous vice president had kept from everyone, including his wife. Humphrey said he had urged Johnson to stay in the race, and he praised Johnson as one of the country's greatest presidents. The vice president wouldn't say what his own plans were. In his memoir, *The Education of a Public Man*, Humphrey said that Muriel was so upset that she went upstairs and wept. "Part of the reason for Muriel's tears was concern for me, for us," he wrote. "Part was resentment that there had been no warning for us that permitted rational planning."[12]

Then we all proceeded into an almost surreal event—a black-tie dinner with the Mexican president, most of his cabinet, and much of

---

12 *The Education of a Public Man*, p. 359.

the Mexican parliament. The mood was artificial and stiff. Humphrey talked calmly with Ordaz, while everyone else was digesting the startling news from Johnson and quietly speculating about what was to come.

When the dinner finally ended, Humphrey gathered several of us back at our hotel. We assumed that he would run for president, but the question was how to proceed in the near term. From Washington, Bill Connell kept trying to reach Humphrey and finally got through. He argued that Humphrey should start calling his old allies, such as George Meany of the AFL-CIO and Walter Reuther of the United Automobile Workers. Connell warned that Bobby Kennedy was already on the phone locking up primaries. "Bill, I'm not calling any of them," the vice president said. "They all know me. They're my friends. If they have something to say to me, they'll contact me."

After we returned to Washington, Humphrey remained publicly uncommitted, though he and his allies engaged in a lot of behind-the-scenes discussion and planning. The assassination of Martin Luther King Jr. on April 4 slowed politics briefly, but Humphrey finally declared that he was in the race on April 27, setting off what would turn out to be a frustrating and deeply flawed campaign.

Cavalier, North Dakota: Where it all began.

The Pembina County Fair held near Cavalier was a major annual event, featuring livestock, baking, farm equipment and games for children. A monkey beat me in a banana-eating contest.

Austria 1956: After my first year at Harvard, before beginning a Fulbright year in England, I divided my time between a French language course in Pau, France, and hitchhiking across Europe, a life-changing experience.

With Ambassador Averell Harriman and Vice President Hubert Humphrey, returning from the first Vietnam trip in February 1966. *Credit: ASSOCIATED PRESS*

Former Vice President Hubert Humphrey in 1972 with my children and Sister M. Celine Hynes, RSM (Sisters of Mercy), who stepped in heroically when needed.

The former vice president visited the Chicago Council on Foreign Relations in 1975.

With my children and Henry Kissinger at the Chicago Council in March 1976. Facing the camera from left: Cathy, Mary Ellen, Tom. John is turned. Sister Celine stands at the far left.

Edith Cresson, French Minister of Trade and Tourism, presented me the Legion d'Honneur in May 1985.

With former German Chancellor Willy Brandt following Brandt's address to the Chicago Council in October 1982.

In 1983, Chicago PBS news anchor John Calloway, right, talked with Jim Hoge, left, the editor of the *Chicago Sun-Times*, and me, center, about the Council's public opinion survey results. (The woman at the table is unidentified.)

Irene and I married on August 1, 1987, surrounded by my children: John, Mary Ellen, Tom and Cathy.

With my mother, Mary, my sister, Mary, and brothers Jim (left) and Bernie in the early 1990s.

In autumn 1991, Irene and I were received by Japanese Prime Minister Kiichi Miyazawa on his first day in office in Tokyo.

With President George H. W. Bush in May 1992 at a White House state dinner for Chilean President Patricio Allwyn.

Our "Thirty-Year Club" of presidents of foreign policy institutes: Karl Kaiser of Germany, Thierry de Montbrial of France and Cesare Merlini of Italy. We gathered at the Atlantic Conference in St. Paul de Vence in November 1986.

Welcoming Mikhail Gorbachev to speak to an overflow crowd at the Chicago Council in May 1992.

On a Council Board of Directors trip to South Africa in February 1996, we had dinner at the Rand Club in Cape Town; left to right, Gavin Relly, CEO Anglo American Corp.; Chicago Council vice chairman Shirley Welsh Ryan; and chairman John Bryan. The painting in the background is of Cecil Rhodes.

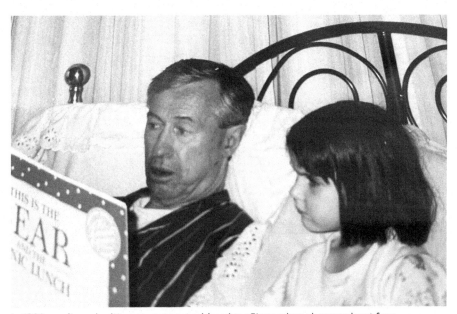

In 1998, reading a bedtime story to granddaughter Fiona when she was about four.

Welcoming Margaret Thatcher to address the Chicago Council in June 1991.
Credit: Chicago Sun-Times Collection, Chicago History Museum

With former German Chancellor Helmut Kohl after he addressed the Council in 2000.

Sharing conversation and laughs in Paris in 2005 with longtime Chicago friend Jeff Shields.

Celebrating my 75th birthday in December 2007.

My very close friend John Manley speaking at my 75th birthday party.

Playing tennis with grandchildren Jason and Riley Hellinger in La Jolla at Christmas 2005.

CHAPTER 9
CAMPAIGNING UNDER LBJ'S THUMB

Humphrey announced his candidacy at the Shoreham Hotel in Washington, speaking of the "politics of happiness" and the "politics of joy," words that were roundly scorned by his opponents and by media commentators given the unrest in the country and the death toll in Vietnam. Of course, I supported his candidacy, but I couldn't help reflecting on how far his career had descended from a time when he arguably did practice the politics of happiness.

With his staunch defense of Johnson's aggressive war policy, Humphrey's credibility with the public had plummeted. When pressed on his views, he could at times be testy and defensive. The media speculated widely that he was hiding his true feelings about Vietnam, and many commentators derided him as a Johnson sycophant. George Lois famously created a cover of *Esquire* magazine in November 1966 showing Humphrey as a dummy sitting on Johnson's lap.umph

That image contrasted sharply with the Humphrey I'd worked with in his late Senate years when he had a powerful legislative role and moved with confidence and spoke his mind. One of the indispensable qualities of a good president is a sense of security—enough self-confidence that he or she can make decisions, stick by them, and not be threatened. Humphrey, I think, had always harbored insecurities, but his successful Senate career had bolstered his self-esteem. In my judgment, he was far better prepared to be president in 1964 than in 1968.

LBJ's banishment had tormented Humphrey, and he craved to be back in the inner circle. He rarely spoke of his situation at the time, but those of us who worked with him could see it in his deflated manner and his eagerness to jump at Johnson's call. The lack of independence and authority in the vice presidency would diminish almost any seasoned politician. Having the manipulative and cruel Lyndon Johnson as a boss only aggravated the problem for Humphrey.

Going back to my early days with Humphrey, I'd had the impression that he shared my view that American military might wouldn't solve the conflict in Vietnam. That's one reason why his advocacy for Johnson's policy during and after the Asia trip was so disheartening to many of us who knew him well. But as the war effort continued to stall, and particularly after the Tet Offensive, the vice president grew slightly more outspoken—on a few occasions indicating that he thought the Vietnam policy should change. He never said anything to me, but he reportedly suggested a complete bombing halt to Johnson—the Rolling Thunder bombing raids on North Vietnam had continued almost unabated since 1965. LBJ again rebuffed him. In several media interviews, Humphrey indicated that if he were in charge, his approach to Vietnam would differ from Johnson's. For the most part, however, he continued to hold to the president's hard line.

Meantime, the negotiation initiative announced by Johnson in his March 31 speech was going nowhere. Starting in May at meetings in Paris, the American representatives, Averell Harriman and Cyrus Vance, held bickering talks with representatives of North Vietnam. The South Vietnamese weren't directly involved, and Saigon insisted that the Viet Cong not participate. While the sides argued, Johnson's bombing raids continued, although with a somewhat reduced scope.

Humphrey went at the presidential campaign with his usual vigor, lining up supporters, campaigning around the country. He wanted to talk about the substantial domestic accomplishments of the Johnson-Humphrey administration, but he understood, somewhat belatedly, that the election would hinge on Vietnam. In his campaign appearances and press interviews, the discussions almost always turned back to the war.

On the Democratic side, Humphrey faced two opponents—Robert Kennedy and Gene McCarthy. Both grounded their campaigns on similar anti-war positions and were battling each other in primaries in states around the country. Humphrey had joined the race basically too late to enter primaries, but because in those days many delegates were controlled by local politicians, he held a strong position. His popularity with labor and years of supporting Democratic candidates, local and national, had earned him enormous goodwill, which readily translated into delegate votes.

Looking ahead, the likely Republican presidential candidate would be Richard Nixon, who was trouncing his primary opponents, principally Nelson Rockefeller and Ronald Reagan, and who had himself collected delegates with his campaign work over the years. Throughout the primaries and fall campaign, Nixon remained cagily ambiguous about his views on Vietnam policy, speaking vaguely of an unspecified plan for an "honorable" solution. The GOP party plank, largely directed by Nixon, called for new leadership and criticized the Johnson administration's "piecemeal" commitment of troops and equipment, but it stayed away from specifics. Campaigning, Nixon focused on bringing "law and order" to the troubled country.

Yet another candidate, former Alabama Governor George Wallace, was running for president on the American Independent Party ticket, basing his campaign on an anti-Black, state's rights platform. His vice presidential candidate, retired General Curtis LeMay, set off a furor in the fall by suggesting the use of nuclear weapons in Vietnam.

Just over six weeks after Humphrey had announced his candidacy, Sirhan Sirhan assassinated Robert Kennedy in the kitchen of the Ambassador Hotel in Los Angeles, shortly after Kennedy celebrated his victory over McCarthy in the California primary. By several accounts, McCarthy was particularly shaken by the murder. The columnists Roland Evans and Robert Novak reported that the senator blamed the death in part on the churning and angry American political process.[13] Just days after Kennedy's death, McCarthy visited Humphrey in his Senate office and, according to Humphrey biographer Arnold A.

---

13 Evans, Roland, and Robert Novak, *"Inside Report: McCarthy Slows But Won't Stop,"* Boston Globe, June 9, 1968.

Offner,[14] offered to withdraw in Humphrey's favor if the vice president would speak out against the war. Humphrey must have been torn. McCarthy's support would have provided an enormous boost, both in gaining the nomination and winning the race in November. But Humphrey's loyalty to Johnson prevailed, and he told McCarthy no. After that, McCarthy carried on, but his campaign sagged.

Senator George McGovern of South Dakota entered the Democratic contest as another anti-war candidate, but his campaign never gathered steam. A number of Democrats, notably Chicago Mayor Richard Daley, urged Teddy Kennedy to pick up the torch, but Kennedy—stunned by the murder of yet another brother and conscious of the demands on him as the patriarch of the large Kennedy clan—declined to run.

That left Humphrey the likely Democratic nominee. As in the '64 campaign when Humphrey was the vice presidential candidate, my first major undertaking was to organize a foreign policy task force to deliver policy recommendations on any substantial issue that might come up. To head the operation, we brought in Zbigniew Brzezinski of Columbia University, whom I had come to know when he was on the Policy Planning Council at the State Department and who had contributed to the task force in the '64 campaign. Born in Poland, he had come to Harvard via Canada, and he still spoke with a discernable accent. Though well-known as a hawk on the Soviet Union, he was generally regarded as a centrist on foreign policy. At the State Department from 1966 to 1968, he had originally supported the military venture in Vietnam. But as President Johnson continued to escalate the military commitment, Brzezinski turned against the war and shortly after joined the Humphrey campaign.

Brzezinski and I brought in other experts to produce papers on issues around the globe—among the experts were Joseph Slater of the Ford Foundation to lead the European Task Force, Marshall Shulman of Columbia to handle arms control, and Doak Barnett of Columbia to oversee China.

By far the most important group was the Vietnam Task Force. To head it, we enlisted Sam Huntington, a renowned political scientist from Harvard and a close friend of Brzezinski's. Huntington was considered to have a conservative global outlook, and, like

---

14 *Hubert Humphrey*, p. 282.

Brzezinski, Huntington had initially supported the war. But he had grown disillusioned with the American effort. Also on the Vietnam Task Force were several Asian experts, including Edwin Reischauer, who had been Kennedy's ambassador to Japan, and Lucian Pye, an authority on China from MIT.

Humphrey was under enormous pressure from his campaign aides and friends to make a break with Johnson over the war. His support for the president's aggressive military approach not only prevented him from picking up Democratic anti-war support but continued to cast him as a Johnson lackey. At some point that summer, I suggested to Humphrey that we let the Vietnam Task Force prepare a speech for him that, if he agreed with its content, would outline how his policy, as president, would differ from Johnson's. He could then either give the speech or present the document to the Democratic platform committee as the basis for a plank in the party platform.

Humphrey agreed. Huntington wrote up a first draft, and then Brzezinski and I both put a hand to edits. The task was delicate; while Humphrey's statement needed to separate him from Johnson's policy, we didn't want the comments to go so far as to infuriate Johnson. We ended up with a relatively short document that emphasized peace rather than a military victory. It called for a negotiated settlement, a reduction in troops, and a promise to stop the bombing of North Vietnam entirely—already reduced after Johnson's March 31 announcement—if the North Vietnamese and Viet Cong showed signs of restraint.

In mid-July, we brought members of the Vietnam Task Force down to Washington to look over the speech for final revisions, and then we met as a group with Humphrey in his congressional office. The co-chairmen of Humphrey's campaign, Senators Walter Mondale of Minnesota and Fred Harris of Oklahoma, joined us, as did Humphrey's longtime friend Secretary of Agriculture Orville Freeman and Ted Van Dyk, who was taking an increasing role in campaign strategy. The vice president read the speech and we went over it with him for about half an hour. In the end, he said he was pleased with the content.

Then Reischauer, a calm, soft-spoken man, asked, "Mr. Vice President, you say you are pleased with the statement. What are you going to do with it?"

"Well, Ed," Humphrey said, "I'm going to show it to the secretary of state."

"What are you gonna do that for?" Reischauer asked in uncharacteristic alarm. "You know what he will say."

Humphrey was taken aback. "I'm the vice president," he said. "I'm at least obligated to show it to the president."

No one argued with that.

Humphrey asked me to make a few minor changes in the document, titled "Toward a Political Settlement and Peace in Southeast Asia," and he made an appointment to see Johnson at 6:00 the next evening.

Van Dyk and I knew this was not a visit Humphrey was looking forward to, so we stopped in at the vice president's office the next day a bit before 6:00, just to check in. "Go home," Humphrey told us. "If anything happens tonight that you need to know, I'll give you a call."

We didn't hear anything, so the next day, when Humphrey came into the office, I asked him what had happened. "Well, I got over there, there were a lot of people around," he said, "and I never did get a chance to go over this alone with the president."

I was skeptical but said we would find another date for the meeting. For the next month or so, Van Dyk and I carried copies of the speech around. As head of communications, Van Dyk was almost always with Humphrey on the campaign plane, and I rode along on several occasions. But somehow the calendars of the president and vice president never coincided enough for them to have that private meeting.

Meantime, Reischauer leaked news of the task force effort to his friend James Reston of *The New York Times*. In late July, Reston wrote a column headlined "Washington: The Savage Pressures of the Campaign," in which he described how Humphrey was getting conflicting views from his advisers—one faction saying the North Vietnamese appeared to be poised for compromise, while another said the enemy was preparing a major offensive. Reston said it remained to be seen which view the vice president would adopt.

Later, well into the fall campaign, I learned what had actually happened at that visit to the White House. Humphrey did get time alone with Johnson and read him the speech. The president listened quietly. At the end, he asked, "Hubert, what are you going to do with that?" Humphrey said he would either give it as a speech or pass it along to the platform committee as the basis for a party plank. A long silence followed, as Humphrey reported. Then Johnson exploded: "God damn it, Hubert, if you give that speech, I will go on national television and denounce you! I'll say you've got the blood of my two sons-in-law, who are in Vietnam, on your hands! John Connelly controls 400 votes at that convention. You won't get a God-damn one of them!" Johnson went on in a rage for seven or eight minutes. Stopping the bombing would jeopardize American troops. The vice president's statement would undermine the Paris peace talks. By the end, Humphrey was so shaken he didn't even tell Muriel what had happened. (He did confess shortly after the encounter to Van Dyk, but Van Dyk kept the secret, only confiding to me later that fall.)

Richard Nixon won the Republican nomination on August 8 at the GOP convention in Miami Beach. A few days later, Brzezinski got a phone call from Henry Kissinger, whom Brzezinski knew from Harvard. Kissinger was still in Harvard's government department, and he had been advising Nelson Rockefeller in his failed race for the Republican nomination. Kissinger now told Brzezinski that he hated Richard Nixon. What's more, Kissinger continued, he had been a longtime admirer of Senator and Vice President Hubert Humphrey and he would like to be helpful in the campaign.

Brzezinski asked what he had in mind, and Kissinger said the Rockefeller staff had been keeping tabs on Nixon for years and compiled a voluminous file. Kissinger had copies of the reports in his office in Cambridge. "There's a lot of damaging material in that file," the professor said. He suggested that either Brzezinski or I come by the office and take a look—the material was at our disposal. Brzezinski thanked him and said he would run it by Humphrey and get back to Kissinger soon. I checked with Humphrey, who said fine, go ahead. So Brzezinski called Kissinger, thanked him for the offer, and said that one of us would stop by in Cambridge.

Throughout that summer, Brzezinski was living in Bar Harbor, Maine, and every other week or so he would come to Washington to help with the campaign. It made sense for him to make the stop in Cambridge. But August turned into September, and he hadn't looked at the file, so I got on his case. Finally, in late September, he planned to make the stop and called Kissinger's office to set up a date. The professor wasn't in, so Brzezinski explained his mission to the secretary. There was a long pause. Finally, she said, "Dr. Brzezinski,

I will of course inform Dr. Kissinger of your call. But you know, of course, he's now working for Mr. Nixon." Needless to say, we never saw that file.

Years later, while investigative reporter Seymour Hersh was researching his book on Kissinger, he got wind of Kissinger's flipped allegiance in the campaign. Hersh talked to Huntington, Brzezinski, Van Dyk, and me and got the full story. Kissinger worried about what might come out and talked to his friend David Rockefeller about finding ways to discredit Hersh's account. Rockefeller knew that his friend Dwayne Andreas, the longtime CEO of Archer Daniels Midland, the huge food processor, had been a Humphrey supporter for years. Rockefeller asked Andreas if he could help. Andreas knew me, so he called. By then, I had a good idea of what Hersh was going to write. When Andreas explained his mission, I had to tell him that Hersh had the story right.

The Hersh book, *The Price of Power: Kissinger in the Nixon White House*, which came out in 1983, mercilessly attacked the former national security chief, but Hersh's account of Kissinger's forsaking of the Humphrey campaign was accurate.[15]

Nonetheless, Humphrey later became an admirer of Kissinger. After Humphrey returned to the Senate in 1971, he worked closely with Kissinger on arms-control issues and détente. In 1973, after visiting the White House, Humphrey told reporters that if he had been elected, he would have appointed Kissinger national security adviser. I doubt it. I don't think Humphrey had even met Kissinger by the time of the 1968 election. Humphrey's bubbling 1973 declaration probably just grew from his enthusiasm for his new friend. In any case, the admiration was mutual. At a dinner years later for the board of a U.S.-German press organization, I sat next to Kissinger, and he went on and on about how he and Humphrey were great friends.

The Democratic National Convention was scheduled for the last week of August in Chicago. I went out a few days early to help advise the platform committee, which would be deciding on a plank on the war, easily the most pressing issue in the campaign. The situation was raw. From the little that was known, the Paris peace talks were stalled, and Johnson was growing increasingly frustrated. Any vague hopes that the Soviet Union might pressure the North Vietnamese

---

15 Hersh, Seymour, *The Price of Power*, Summit Books (1983), p. 14.

to cooperate ended on August 20 when Soviet troops marched into Czechoslovakia to suppress a liberalization movement. Meantime, the call had gone out for anti-war protestors to descend on Chicago during the convention.

The chairman of the platform committee was Hale Boggs, a Louisiana representative and warm supporter of Johnson's Vietnam policy. LBJ had insisted throughout that the Democrats must not declare a departure from his strategy. Still, the anti-war delegates—representing the Kennedy/McCarthy/McGovern faction—comprised a substantial headcount on the platform committee, though less than a majority. Their advocates before the committee included several prominent doves who had roots in the Kennedy administration: Richard Goodwin, Pierre Salinger, and Ted Sorensen.

Humphrey had enlisted a seasoned Washington lawyer, David Ginsburg, to represent his interests with the committee. The two of them went back years together to the early days of the ADA. Ginsburg had recently been in the news as director of the Kerner Commission, examining the riots that had been tearing apart the nation's cities. The commission had released its report just months before, famously declaring that the country was "moving toward two societies, one black, one white—separate and unequal."

I didn't participate directly in the committee's deliberations, but I was available to confer with Ginsburg whenever a question came up. Ginsburg pressed for a plank that would break with Johnson but not so broadly as to incite him—basically, a middle road between the anti-war faction and Johnson's supporters. In the end, Ginsburg compromised with the Kennedy/McCarthy/McGovern faction on a proposed plank that essentially followed the same prescription as set out in the speech that the Humphrey task force had written, including the call for a bombing halt. It soon came to be known as the "peace plank."

Still pained by Johnson's reaction to his proposed speech, Humphrey ran the language of the peace plank past Rusk and National Security Adviser Walt Rostow. Both said it was acceptable. But LBJ got wind of the plank and summoned Hale Boggs to Washington. Johnson said the peace plank had to go—he would never agree to a unilateral bombing halt, which he insisted would risk the lives of American soldiers. When Boggs gave the committee the president's orders, Humphrey called Johnson at his ranch in Texas. Johnson was "immovable," as Humphrey later wrote in his memoir.[16]

So Humphrey agreed on a plank that was widely viewed as a signal of support for the current administration policy. In the hindsight of history, the difference in language between the peace plank and Johnson's plank seems so nuanced and slight as to make one wonder what all the arguing was about. But such was the tenor of the times, and the media treated the difference as substantial. The principal conflict came over the bombing. The peace plank called for an outright halt. The Johnson-approved language said the bombing would stop only when it wouldn't endanger lives in the field.

The doves treated the difference as a line in the sand and refused to support the tougher version. The peace plank lost in the committee and later, when it was presented as a minority plank to the convention at large, it lost in a vote among all the delegates, a decision that fueled the rowdy protests in Chicago's streets. Humphrey's hopes to carve an identity apart from current administration policy were dashed. "Now I know, in retrospect, that I should have stood my ground," Humphrey wrote.

Humphrey won the nomination on the first ballot. He made repeated unsuccessful efforts to sign up Ted Kennedy as his running mate and ultimately selected Edmund Muskie, the Maine senator. I knew Muskie only slightly but considered him a solid politician and a good choice.

A number of people had been working on Humphrey's acceptance speech, which was expected to draw substantial attention, given the conflicts within the party and the increasing clashes between Chicago police and protesters. But the drafting process proved as chaotic as the convention itself. Humphrey brought in any number of people to advise on the text, from representatives of labor to his personal physician. At one session to go over the speech, I recall 15 or 16 people in the room. I finally just withdrew from the tangled task. Humphrey eventually delivered a speech that was a weak mishmash and widely disdained.

The convention ended after four tumultuous days. I was little touched by the battles in the streets, though occasionally the air where I worked or slept was tinged with the acidy odor of tear gas

---

16 *The Education of a Public Man*, p. 389.

or smoke bombs. But for those of us in the Humphrey camp, it was impossible to leave without a feeling of deep gloom. I couldn't imagine how the event could have gone worse for the vice president.

CHAPTER 10
TOO LITTLE, TOO LATE

A nationwide Gallup poll on September 11 had Humphrey trailing Nixon by 12 points (43% to 31%, with George Wallace drawing 19%). I thought it was over for the vice president. Larry O'Brien, an old JFK hand, had been brought in to manage the Humphrey campaign, and he, as well as other advisers, felt the same way. They argued that Humphrey only stood a chance if he broke dramatically with Johnson's Vietnam policy.

Humphrey refused to do it. He floated a ready excuse—though the Paris peace talks seemed to be going nowhere, the vice president told aides he didn't want to step on a possible breakthrough. But his real reason was his fear of Johnson's wrath. When he made tentative public remarks about stopping the bombing, Johnson berated him in a phone call and then gave a speech to the American Legion in New Orleans defending his policy and giving an unsubtle reprimand to Humphrey. Reports floated out that Johnson regularly disparaged Humphrey behind his back. Indeed, by some accounts, Johnson thought that Nixon was more likely to sustain an aggressive approach to the war, and hence the president wanted Nixon to win.

Remarkably, Humphrey's loyalty to Johnson almost never cracked. Occasionally, he would make a glancing remark to the effect that the president wasn't doing him any favors. Ted Van Dyk reported that once during the campaign, after being rebuked by Johnson yet again, Humphrey grumbled, "I've eaten so much of Johnson's shit in this job that I've grown to like the taste of it." But the vice president was so paranoid about his comments getting back to Johnson that he almost never complained.

Gene McCarthy wasn't doing Humphrey any favors, either. Though Humphrey stood as the only reasonable choice for doves among the three candidates, McCarthy had left for France after the convention and refused to endorse the Democratic candidate.

By late September, Gallup reported that Nixon's lead with voters had grown to 15 points, and even George Wallace was gaining ground on the vice president. Humphrey finally recognized that he would lose the election unless he signaled a departure from Johnson. The strongest catalyst for the break came from George Ball, who had lobbied against the war internally within the Johnson administration. After leaving the State Department in 1966, Ball joined Lehman Brothers, but in June 1968, Johnson had muscled him into taking the role of ambassador to the United Nations.

Ball resigned that post barely three months later and joined Humphrey on the campaign trail. An Adlai Stevenson disciple going back to Illinois, Ball liked Humphrey and wanted him to win. More than that, Ball passionately hated Nixon. I think he assumed the election of Nixon would be a disaster for the country. Ball and Larry O'Brien went to work on Humphrey and finally persuaded him that his only chance to win the election—by now a slim one— was to break publicly with Johnson. Ball had quietly checked with Averell Harriman in Paris, who allowed that a slight shift from the administration's hard line would not hinder the talks.

The campaign bought television time on the evening of September 30 on an NBC affiliate in Salt Lake City, where the vice president was scheduled to campaign. The speech drew from the task force report and was largely written by Ball, O'Brien, and Humphrey with a polish by Van Dyk. The separation from Johnson was subtle, the language carefully crafted. Again, the salient point concerned the bombing. Humphrey said as president he would take an "acceptable risk for peace" and would halt the bombing entirely, though he added he would closely monitor the actions of the North Vietnamese.

Just before the broadcast, Humphrey called Johnson and read him the speech. In his memoir,[17] Humphrey recounts that the president listened and then said, "I gather you're not asking my advice."

Humphrey told the president that nothing in the speech would embarrass him or interfere with the Paris talks.

"Thanks for calling, Hubert." The call ended. Johnson only spoke out for Humphrey at the close of the campaign, and the president gave many indications that he favored Nixon.

In the flurry of reporting around Humphrey's broadcast, the campaign staff suggested that the vice president's policy went well beyond the administration's. Press secretary Norman Sherman, for example, pointed out that the statement had not been cleared by the White House.

Overall, the speech drew a mixed response from the media. Johnny Apple, in his story in *The New York Times*, suggested that Humphrey's stance differed hardly at all from Johnson's, and Apple cited several instances when LBJ had made essentially the same point about the bombing. Joseph Kraft in *The Washington Post*, on the other hand, argued that the speech had ignited the Humphrey campaign. "[W]hile the words are not very impressive, the music—the buildup of them; the fine counterpoint with the White House and Richard Nixon, and the orchestration of reaction—suggests something important."

In any case, the public took the speech as a sign that Humphrey was at last escaping "the fatal embrace" of Johnson, as Kraft put it. Humphrey's poll numbers immediately began to climb, and he steadily narrowed the gap with Nixon. Throughout the campaign, I privately thought that Humphrey had inflicted so much damage on himself that he could never win, but the speech ignited my hopes.

Behind the scenes, however, Henry Kissinger was busy tilting the scales toward Nixon. According to Walter Isaacson's 1992 biography *Kissinger*,[18] the Harvard professor let the Nixon campaign team know that he was going to visit Paris and offered to provide scuttlebutt from the peace talks. The campaign happily accepted the offer. In Paris, Kissinger met with two young, slightly starstruck members of Averell Harriman's staff. Nothing significant had yet been established, but

---

17 *The Education of a Public Man*, p. 403.
18 Isaacson, Walter, *Kissinger*, Simon & Schuster (1992), pp. 130–132.

Kissinger learned that the talks seemed to be heating up. Kissinger promptly alerted former Attorney General John Mitchell, who was running the Nixon campaign, that Paris could soon yield something substantial.

Several weeks later, the White House announced that the talks had taken a promising turn—Hanoi had indicated that it might meet some of the American terms for halting the bombing. The Nixon camp recognized that a breakthrough in the talks would provide an enormous boost to Humphrey. By this time, Nixon and his aides had found an ally in Anna Chennault, the Chinese-born widow of an American Air Force general. Chennault was a prominent Republican and a well-connected social figure in both Washington and Saigon. In particular, she was close to the South Vietnamese ambassador in Washington, Bui Diem.

In late October, just days before the election, Mitchell told her that a breakthrough in the negotiations was imminent, and he emphasized that the South Vietnamese government would get a much better deal if Nixon were president. Chennault alerted Bui Diem to the clear implication: Don't agree to participate in negotiations until after the election. The ambassador passed the information to Thieu and Ky, and progress toward negotiations stalled.

As it turned out, the FBI was tapping the phone of the South Vietnamese ambassador and overheard the conversation between Bui Diem and Madame Chennault. J. Edgar Hoover passed a copy of the tape to President Johnson.

What the Nixon camp was doing was outrageous and arguably treasonous—trying to impede a negotiation that could end the war. Johnson worried that if he revealed the treachery, he would be accused of trying to influence the election. So rather than act himself on the information, the president told the candidates what he had learned. He essentially let Nixon and Humphrey decide what to do. Nixon falsely denied any knowledge of the plot, but, of course, he wanted the whole thing quiet and buried—the news would certainly torpedo his campaign. But Humphrey also decided to keep silent. He worried that publicizing the Nixon camp's actions would sabotage the peace talks and likely end any hope of serious negotiations. He didn't want that on his shoulders. (He never alerted his staff to the situation.)

Humphrey also recognized that an announcement of that magnitude this close to the end of the campaign—accusing Nixon of treason, even if Humphrey didn't use that word—would utterly disrupt the election and could seriously undermine the voters' confidence in the democratic process. Still, Humphrey recounts in his memoir thinking on election day, "I wonder if I should have blown the whistle on Anna Chennault and Nixon."[19]

Details on the Nixon camp's dirty work have surfaced over the years, but some facts emerged early on. In his 1969 book on the election, the celebrated campaign reporter Theodore H. White said of Humphrey's decision to stay silent: "I know of no more essentially decent story in American politics."[20] Humphrey's silence stands in particularly stark contrast to the actions of Donald Trump and other top Republicans during and after the 2020 election, actions that unleashed chaos and violence and that tested the faith of many Americans in the country's elections.

On October 31, five days before the election, President Johnson went on television to announce that he had seen enough hints of accommodation from North Vietnam that he was calling a bombing halt. Johnson was basically following the course Humphrey had been urging, though he didn't cast his decision that way and went so far as to demand that Humphrey not take any credit for the change in policy. But Johnson followed up by campaigning for Humphrey for the first time.

The polls continued to narrow, and by election day, November 5, those of us in Humphrey's camp could hope that he might eke out a victory. We gathered at the Leamington Hotel in Minneapolis. By midnight, the results were clear. The popular vote was close—less than 1% of votes cast—but Nixon had won with a substantial advantage in the Electoral College, 301 to 191.

The autopsies of the Humphrey campaign began immediately and have continued to this day. Many Humphrey supporters blamed Johnson, not only for his humiliation of the vice president over the years but specifically for his failure to support him in the campaign until the last minute. The president still carried weight with many Americans, and if he had spoken out even a month earlier, the votes

---

[19] *The Education of a Public Man*, p. 8.
[20] White, Theodore H., *The Making of the President 1968*, Atheneum (1969), p. 381.

might have swung Humphrey's way. Other Humphrey supporters bitterly faulted Gene McCarthy. After Humphrey won the nomination, the anti-war crusader said he would back Humphrey, but then he decamped for Europe. Even after he returned, he stalled and didn't come out for Humphrey until a few weeks before the election. Again, if McCarthy had weighed in earlier, he might have made a difference.

But the real blame for the loss belonged to Humphrey himself. He had squandered his standing among many Americans with his dutiful support of Johnson's Vietnam policy. Even so, he might have overcome his handicap if he had broken with Johnson earlier in the campaign, as so many of his advisers had been urging from the start. Yet he failed to act until George Ball and Larry O'Brien finally pressured him to speak out.

Six months after the election, Humphrey asked me to join him for a drink in Washington—I think it was at the Hay-Adams Hotel. By then, he had settled into a cushy consulting job with Encyclopedia Britannica, run by his friend William Benton. Humphrey had been devastated by his loss in the election, but he'd rebounded, and he looked good. A year later, he would recapture his Senate seat from Minnesota.

As we sipped drinks, he brought up his reluctance to break with Johnson on Vietnam. "I know you were disappointed, John, as were a number of your colleagues on the staff," he said. "And I have spent a great deal of time and a number of sleepless nights over the last six months thinking about why I acted as I did. And the best explanation I can come up with—and it's not an adequate explanation, but the best I can come up with—is that after four years as Lyndon Johnson's vice president, I'd become like the oldest son, and I couldn't break the tie." And then Humphrey repeated, "I'd become like the oldest son and couldn't break the tie."

And that was pretty much the end of that discussion.

CHAPTER 11
ON THE ROAD FOR FORD

Humphrey's loss in the election didn't surprise me, though I was sorry—both for the country and for myself. In my optimistic moments, I had imagined having a significant foreign policy role in a Humphrey administration. With the defeat, I turned my focus elsewhere. But for reasons that I have never fully understood, Elizabeth was gravely disappointed at Humphrey's defeat. She had been busy raising our children and hadn't participated in the campaign, and I'd never detected in her a preternatural dislike for Nixon. Still, her unhappiness was the first serious sign of a coming rupture in our family. Our daughter Mary Ellen recalled, "Humphrey's loss was monumental. I think the sadness of this sort of settled over all of us for quite a number of years."

Meantime, I had to find a new job. I got calls from people who offered condolences and provided suggestions, including David Rockefeller, whom I had come to know while working on the Alliance for Progress. Within a few weeks, I had meetings with Rockefeller, IBM, Citibank, and the Dreyfus Fund, among other businesses, but I knew I wasn't cut out for corporate or finance work, and academia seemed a bit quiet for my temperament at that point. I was better suited for an NGO or foundation.

The Ford Foundation, now headed by McGeorge Bundy, was the most influential foundation in the world in those days. Bundy had been there since early 1966, when he signaled his interest in the job and left the White House. Joe Slater, who had earlier talked to me about working at Ford, had left by then, but I knew Dave Bell, the head of Ford's international division (who likely would have been named president if Bundy hadn't suddenly said he was available). Bell had been budget director for President Kennedy and later head of the Agency for International Development, where I had worked with him as a member of Senator Humphrey's staff.

I got in touch with Bell, and he invited me up to Ford's New York headquarters for interviews, which went well. As the head of a family with four kids and no trust fund, I told the foundation I couldn't afford to take a job in New York. Ford was planning to open a European office, which would have been an ideal job for me, but the foundation was already well on the way to hiring someone for the position. So Ford offered me a job as a full-time consultant on European affairs, which I assumed would only last a year or two. Either a suitable foreign position with the foundation would come up or I would move on.

I ended up splitting my time between New York and Washington. I'd take the train or fly up on Monday morning, stay overnight at the Harvard Club, then return to D.C. late Tuesday. In Washington, Ford had arranged for me to have an office at the Brookings Institution, which was a Ford client.

My first major Ford project was a trip to Europe, arranged principally to acquaint me with the foundation's contacts and projects there. I visited France, England, Germany, Italy, and Switzerland, among other countries. Ford employees traveled well in those days, so I enjoyed first-class tickets and luxury hotels.

That trip had another purpose, one that shines a light on a significant battleground of the Cold War. Since the founding of the CIA after World War II, the Ford Foundation had maintained a professional relationship with the spy agency. Shepard Stone, the head of Ford's International Division from 1952 to 1967, was the principal link with the CIA. He knowingly worked closely on some agency projects, especially operations that pushed back against Soviet influence among students and intellectuals.

The Soviets made no apologies for supporting efforts to press their agenda, particularly in Europe. And most local communist parties got financial support from the Soviets and held to the Soviet line. The communists often found fertile ground in Western Europe, not simply because of ideology, but also because many European elites resented American power and derided our commercial culture.

With the onset of the Cold War, Washington wanted to counteract Soviet influence but also was coy about its activities, as in the case of its secretive support of the National Student Association. Any initiative with the overt backing of the U.S. government would likely get a hostile reception in Europe. And likewise, many American artists and academics who otherwise might participate in international exchanges would hesitate if they thought they would be part of a government propaganda scheme. So the CIA silently partnered with like-minded civilian operations, such as the Ford Foundation.[21] To this day, I don't fault the CIA or Ford for trying to promote democratic values against Soviet efforts to push Soviet influence.

One of the foremost CIA vehicles was the Congress for Cultural Freedom (CCF), which supported a range of pro-American journals and projects, many aimed particularly at educated elites in the Communist Bloc. At Ford, Shepard Stone supported funding for the CCF. But revelations in the late 1960s in *The New York Times*, *Ramparts*, and elsewhere about the CIA connection dealt the organization a severe blow. The CCF ended its ties with the CIA. To prevent the organization's demise, Bundy stepped forward and pledged a five-year, $25 million grant to the renamed International Association for Cultural Freedom. Stone left Ford and took over as the Association's head.

On my trip to Europe for Ford, I was supposed to assess whether the renamed organization was still effective and worthy of Ford support. In the end, my report to Ford was largely negative. "[F]ew people with whom I spoke believe that the Association can be today an effective instrument for contact with the intellectual and professional elites of the countries of Eastern Europe and the Soviet Union. . . ." I added, "If the International Association for Cultural Freedom has deep roots among the younger generation (i.e., 20-40) in any of the Western European countries, I was unable to find them." I advocated continuing the current (substantially decreased) levels of

---

[21] Volker Berghan, in *America and the Intellectual Cold Wars in Europe* (Princeton, 2001), gives a good account of these operations.

support for the Association but recommended not going beyond the five-year term. (The Association continued to decline and ultimately shut down in the late 1970s.)

On the trip, I also assessed the general state of intellectual and professional elites in Eastern Europe and efforts to reach them from Western Europe. On that front, my assessment was mixed. Some Communist Bloc countries were more open than others—Czechoslovakia (despite the 1968 Soviet crackdown on Prague) and Hungary showed more signs of liberalization than Poland, for example. And the quality of East-West programs was uneven. In retrospect, what stands out in my report is this observation: "Most Western commentators believe that Marxism is no longer taken seriously as an ideology in the countries of Eastern Europe, but is merely a tool for acquisition and exercise of power."

Also at Ford, I got drawn into a messy funding issue faced by a Ford client, a matter that has little historical significance but features a noted scholar and demonstrates how loosely foundations were run at the time. After Adlai Stevenson died suddenly of a heart attack in 1965, a group of his friends set up an institute in his honor. The Adlai Stevenson Institute of International Affairs would deal with pressing global issues. It took the new board of trustees a long time to find a director, and they finally gave the job to William Polk, a University of Chicago professor and the founding head of the school's Center for Middle Eastern Studies.

Polk came from a substantial Texas family. His older brother George was a CBS correspondent murdered in 1948 during the Greek civil war. The prestigious George Polk Awards for outstanding journalism are named in his honor. Bill Polk himself was a recognized scholar of the Middle East trained at Harvard, and he'd served in John Kennedy's State Department. He aspired to become ambassador to Iran or Egypt and thought Vice President Humphrey could help him attain that. He cultivated me with lavish dinners at his big house in Virginia because he hoped I could lead him to Humphrey and that coveted ambassadorship. His presumption was way off. Not only did Humphrey play no role in ambassadorial appointments, but Dean Rusk disliked Polk. So he left for Chicago.

He landed the Adlai Stevenson Institute job after running into an Institute trustee who mentioned the foundation was looking for a director. Polk said he could do the job, along with running the U of

C's Center for Middle Eastern Studies. So he was hired, and as a tax-exempt nonprofit, the Adlai Stevenson Institute fell administratively under the umbrella of the University of Chicago. The organization set up shop in the Robie House, a famous Frank Lloyd Wright building on the edge of the U of C campus.

With Polk as its head, the Institute sponsored seminars, underwrote fellowships, and published the results of its studies. Some of its projects earned attention. In June 1968, for example, it brought together historians and foreign policy experts—Henry Kissinger, Sam Huntington, and Arthur Schlesinger, among them—for a conference titled "No More Vietnams?" The Institute invited representatives for all the potential presidential candidates, so I was there as part of the Humphrey camp. Papers from the conference were published later that year as a well-reviewed book, *No More Vietnams? The War and the Future of American Foreign Policy*, edited by Richard M. Pfeffer.

But Bill Polk liked to live large. In Chicago, he and his then-wife resided in what the *Tribune* described as "an enormous old residence surrounded by grass and trees on two sides and a tennis court at the rear. The house is filled with oriental rugs, and antiques from 'back alleys' of Rome as well as more pretentious places."

As head of the Institute, Polk was not a careful manager of the organization's finances and operations. Neither the Institute's board nor the University of Chicago kept a particularly tight rein on his dealings. In 1967, Polk—who'd earlier written an excellent book on Iran—arranged a $3 million grant from the government of Iran. Most of the money was to go toward building an elaborate home for the Institute and for the Center for Middle Eastern Studies on the U of C campus. The building was to be named the Pahlavi Center in honor of the Shah, who visited Hyde Park in June 1968 for a groundbreaking. Three years later, the building project was dropped, apparently because of rising costs. The university returned $3 million to Iran.

Polk was also casual about awarding fellowships—grants of around $50,000 annually. For example, the former *New York Times* writer David Halberstam ran into Polk in New York and mentioned that he'd run out of money while writing his book about Vietnam, *The Best and the Brightest*. Polk gave him a fellowship on the spot.

At some point in the late 1960s, the Ford Foundation had offered the Institute a $1 million challenge grant—the Institute would get the money if it could raise $2 million on its own within two years.

One of my early tasks at Ford was to go out to Chicago to see how the Institute was doing on the offer. When I arrived, Polk threw me a fancy dinner accompanied by two bottles of $50 wine, at a time when a bottle of $50 wine was extravagant. He readily acknowledged that he employed a car and driver. In interviews with the fellows, I learned that the Halberstam experience was not an aberration—many fellowships were given out with little vetting besides Polk's enthusiasm. Several of the Institute's board members voiced growing concern about Polk's freewheeling ways, and the challenge-grant fund had reached only two-thirds of the $2 million goal.

I ultimately recommended—and Ford agreed—to give the Institute $667,000, but to impose stronger conditions on how the money was spent and how the Institute was run. Meeting with Ford officials in New York, Polk readily agreed but returned to Chicago and casually ignored most of the restrictions.

That's not the end of the saga of Bill Polk and the Adlai Stevenson Institute, but meanwhile I was drawn into a somewhat related crisis at Ford. Reports had surfaced on the excesses of foundations—family members on the payroll, grants to relatives of the founder, hoarding of principal, and so on. Because most private foundations had been set up by a rich person or family, they were often suspected of being vehicles for tax evasion. The House Ways and Means Committee started looking into the foundation business. Under Chairman Wilbur Mills, the committee called witnesses, and McGeorge Bundy of the Ford Foundation was the first to appear.

Bundy's testimony was a disaster. Though he was always cordial to me, he could be coldly imperious, particularly if he thought he was dealing with someone below his intellectual rank. In four and a half hours before the committee, he treated the House members as if they were dim high school sophomores, overexplaining at some points, disdaining questions at others. Some of the conflict had a partisan edge. After the assassination of Robert Kennedy, Bundy had granted Ford money to a handful of Kennedy aides, and some committee members demanded to know how those grants fit within the foundation's charter. Bundy insisted they were "educational" and served for the "development" of the recipients. Other committee members criticized grants for inner-city projects and voter drives. Even grants to assorted congressmen came under fire.

Bundy's appearance seemed to fuel the groundswell of interest in taxing foundations. *The New York Times* quoted Representative John Byrnes, a Wisconsin Republican, as questioning whether "with taxes as high as they are today," Congress could continue tax exemption for foundations when "Foundations have no halo."

The congressional action threatened not only the Ford Foundation but all private foundations. So they fought back with a lobbying campaign under the direction of the lawyer for the Lilly Endowment in Indianapolis. At Ford, my colleague Bill Bader and I, who both had experience with Congress, were pulled into the effort. For 8 or 10 weeks in the summer of 1969, we worked on figuring out how to approach members of Congress—where were the affected foundations, who had influence, how to make the case against heavy taxation. It was a well-organized effort. In the end, the tax law of 1969 imposed some sensible restrictions, such as limiting nepotistic deals and requiring a foundation to spend 5% of assets for charitable purposes each year.

However, one restriction had a particularly worrisome repercussion for Ford and the University of Chicago: Both the foundation making the grant and the nonprofit organization receiving it had so-called "expenditure responsibility." That meant both had to closely monitor the terms of the grant to make sure the money was being spent appropriately or face serious tax consequences. That put the conduct of the Adlai Stevenson Institute in the crosshairs of the law.

Bill Polk raised the stakes. In early 1975, the Lilly Endowment, whose president, Landrum Bolling, was a Middle East expert and a friend of Polk's, gave the Adlai Stevenson Institute $160,000. Polk didn't mention the grant to the Institute's board, but he announced he was leaving the Institute and the university. In the early summer of 1975, he relocated to Cairo, Egypt, renting the "grand" house of the former British ambassador. Several principals involved told me the Lilly money went with him. He may have considered it a severance payment.

The University of Chicago spent more than a year trying to sort through what had happened at the Adlai Stevenson Institute—the school wanted both to stay out of trouble with the IRS and to stay in the good graces of the Ford Foundation, which was a major funder of U of C projects. Chauncey Harris, vice president for international affairs and a renowned geographer, and Professor William H. McNeill, a world-famous historian, spent a total of a year and a half sorting through the records. Eventually, the university satisfied Ford that the grant process was under control. In 1975, the Institute was absorbed into the university, as an announcement put it, and effectively disappeared.

In the next few decades, while largely based in Europe, Bill Polk founded a consulting firm, lectured, and wrote books, several of which were widely admired. I lost track of him until November 1986, when I was at a conference in St. Paul de Vence on France's Cote d'Azur. We had Saturday afternoon off, so I visited the nearby Maeght Foundation, which contains one of the world's foremost sculpture collections. Wandering around the sculpture garden, I bumped into Bill Polk, a beautiful young woman on his arm. She turned out to be his third wife, a baroness.

He greeted me effusively and said he lived nearby. We chatted for several minutes, catching up. Neither of us mentioned his tangled relationship with the Adlai Stevenson Institute. And that was the last I ever saw of him.

Quite inadvertently, though, Bill Polk did me a large favor. When I came out to Chicago in 1969 to look into the Ford grant to the Adlai Stevenson Institute, I came to know some of the city's prominent civic-minded citizens, several of them connected to the Chicago Council on Foreign Relations. Two years later, when the Council was looking for a new executive director, I got a call.

CHAPTER 12
BRINGING THE WORLD TO CHICAGO

I enjoyed working for the Ford Foundation, but because of Humphrey's loss in the 1968 election, I didn't want to remain in Washington long term. Even in those days, Washington was a deeply partisan town, and as a member of Humphrey's staff, I was a marked man. A significant government job wouldn't come up while Republicans held the White House. Returning to a Senate role would be a serious step down. So even while at Ford, I kept my eyes open for opportunities elsewhere. In the spring of 1969, I learned that the Chicago Council on Foreign Relations was looking for an executive director. I sent in a résumé but heard nothing. The organization ended up hiring William Cole, the former president of Lake Forest College in Chicago's north suburbs. The Council leadership acted without interviewing anyone—two members of the Council selection committee were board members of Lake Forest College.

Meantime, after a little over a year at Ford, I was offered a job at the Overseas Development Council, a new organization created by Ford and by the Rockefeller Foundation and headed by James Grant, a former official of the U.S. Agency for International Development (AID). The Development Council's mission was to build support for both public and private development projects underway in needy countries around the world. The work involved organizing seminars, producing publications, and lobbying Congress.

Like the Alliance for Progress, the Overseas Development Council hoped that more sophisticated, diverse economies would change the balance of power in at least some developing nations—an idea I thoroughly endorsed. What's more, the Development Council's offices were just a few blocks down the street from the Brookings Institution, where I had been spending three days a week. A move would be simple, so I took the job.

I hadn't been there a year when I was alerted by several people in Chicago—including then Illinois Treasurer Adlai Stevenson III—that the Chicago Council on Foreign Relations was again looking for an executive director. Bill Cole, the man hired a year before, had clashed with council chairman Alex Seith, who was determined to run the organization himself. It was a classic board/staff clash and left a lot of blood on the floor. To add to the turmoil, Cole was allowed to remain in his office for six months, even though he'd been stripped of his authority. Despite the awkward situation, the job appealed to me.

The Council enjoyed a rich history. (The name changed in 2006 to the Chicago Council on Global Affairs, but for the most part in these pages, I'll simply call it the Council.) A select group of largely wealthy and cosmopolitan Chicagoans from Lake Forest, an elite North Shore suburb, had founded the organization in 1922. The United States had just finished playing a decisive role in World War I, but then sunk into isolationism marked by the failure to join President Woodrow Wilson's League of Nations. Historically, the Midwest had been an anchor of isolationism, its citizens seeing little need to stretch their provincial interests. As a breadbasket and growing center of manufacturing, the Midwestern economy was starting to reach beyond the nation's borders, but the expansion hadn't yet raised strong interest in the outside world among Chicagoans and other Midwesterners.

The Council's founders—William Hale and his sister-in-law Susan Follansbee Hibbard—cared about what was going on in Europe and around the globe. Together with a handful of like-minded associates, they created the Council to nurture their interests and perhaps educate Midwesterners out of their isolationist cocoon. Less than a year after the founding, the Council made its name by playing host to Georges Clemenceau, the former premier of France and a World

War I hero. As the *Tribune* wrote on his arrival, "Georges Clemenceau, the 'Tiger of France,' arrives in Chicago today, and the city awaits his coming with the guns of Argonne ready to fire a salute of welcome." Throngs cheered as Clemenceau's car traveled the streets. He told a packed Council audience in the Auditorium Theater that Germany was still a threat and—no doubt thrilling the Council's founders—he urged Chicagoans to move beyond an isolationist policy.

Over the following decades, the membership remained small—under 3,000—but the Council brought in a distinguished roster of speakers, among them John Maynard Keynes, the British economist, in 1931, and Hiroshi Saito, the Japanese ambassador to the United States, in 1935. Alexander Kerensky, who served briefly as the president of Russia as the revolution was unfolding, addressed the Council in 1927, a period when Chicago was ravaged by gang warfare and run by a clownish mayor, William Hale (Big Bill) Thompson. Writing on the *Tribune*'s society pages, the reporter, "Mme X," said the picture Kerensky painted of Russia today was "vivid and depressing." The reporter added that some people similarly criticized Chicago. "A good cure might be to send them to Russia for a few months."

For much of the 1930s, the Council was run by an astute and energetic young man, Clifton Utley, the father of the future television reporter Garrick Utley. The board chairman from 1935 to 1937 was an up-and-coming Chicago lawyer named Adlai Stevenson II. As Richard C. Longworth writes in his 2021 history of the Council, *Chicago and the World*,[22] the chairman would introduce guest speakers at events, and by several accounts, Stevenson lavished hours on polishing his brief remarks, turning himself from a somewhat awkward public figure to the smart and witty orator of his later campaigns. It was reliably reported that Council members would come just to hear Adlai's introductions.

From the start, the Council chose to be nonpartisan and nonprescriptive—it would present guests with strong political opinions without endorsing or criticizing them. With fascism spreading in Europe, and Germany behaving with increasing belligerence, the Council brought in speakers representing various points of view. After Germany invaded Poland in 1939, American attitudes toward foreign policy divided even more sharply between

---

22 Longworth, Richard C., *Chicago and the World*, Agate Publishing (2021), p. 36.

interventionists and isolationists. "Increasingly, Council speakers talked about what the spread of fascism meant to the US, and what the US should do about it," Longworth writes. "The great debate had begun."[23]

One of the loudest American voices for isolation came from a prominent figure in the Council's backyard: Colonel Robert McCormick, the editor and publisher of the *Chicago Tribune*. For a mixture of reasons—not least, he hated his old Groton schoolmate, President Franklin D. Roosevelt, who was thought to lean to intervention—The Colonel, as he was known, relentlessly pushed the isolationist cause through the pages of his newspaper. From the Council's founding, McCormick never warmed to the organization's gaze beyond the country's shores, and his paper regularly downplayed and even derided Council activities, as Longworth writes.[24] World War II again brought the United States into the wider world, but after the war, the *Tribune* continued to rage against internationalist ideas, such as the United Nations and the Marshall Plan. In a brutal editorial titled "BLOOD ON THEIR HANDS" on December 9, 1950, the *Tribune* wrote, "The purpose of this editorial is to invite some soul searching on the part of the members of the Chicago Council on Foreign Relations. They oughtn't to be looking around for somebody else to blame for the disaster in Korea when they themselves did what they could to bring it about."

The editorial went on to argue that the conflict in Korea was a "direct consequence" of interventionist and internationalist policies that were supported by many Council members. "Thanks to these policies, 300,000 American boys lost their lives in the 1941-45 war, and 5,600 have been listed as killed thus far in Korea."

Council members were naturally peeved and frustrated by McCormick's antagonism, and a legend—apocryphal, but telling—used to circulate in the Council offices: The Colonel had banned the name Utley—as in Clifton Utley, the Council's high-profile executive director—from the pages of the newspaper.

The Colonel died in 1955, but the *Tribune*'s antagonism continued while his acolytes still ran the paper. The Council faced other problems in the 1950s and 1960s, however. With the advent of the

---

23 *Chicago and the World*, p. 40.
24 *Chicago and the World*, pp. 90-91.

Cold War, the nation took a greater interest in foreign affairs, which meant the Council's role as the bearer of foreign news faced increasing competition, particularly from television. Though membership still hovered between 2,000 and 3,000, the organization struggled to remain relevant and, more specifically, to pay for its programs. For a time, it produced a half-hour Sunday television show on Chicago's educational station, but interest faded after a few years. Chairmen and executive directors came and went.

Then, in 1960, strapped for cash and members, the Council hired an advertising man, Edmond Eger, as executive director. He found the recipe for an elixir in the fine print of the rules of the Civil Aeronautics Board, which regulated airlines. Nonprofit organizations—unlike commercial airlines—could run charter flights. At the time, transatlantic travel was just starting to take off. Soon, the Council was offering its members flights to Europe at $300 or so round trip, while Pan American Airlines and others were charging $1,000 or more. The Council wasn't allowed to make a profit on the flights themselves, but membership—$20 annually—soared with eager travelers and soon climbed to close to 20,000.

Before long, this makeshift bonanza was dominating the organization. Soon after I started at the Council, I met a prominent Chicago executive, Tom Coulter, president of the Chicago Association of Commerce and Industry, who asked what I did. I told him I ran a foreign policy organization called the Council on Foreign Relations. He said, "John, that's not a foreign policy organization—that's a travel club." I quickly learned he wasn't entirely wrong.

A serious personnel conflict was also impeding the Council. A smart and ambitious young lawyer, Alex Seith, had risen to Council board chairman in 1968. No doubt influenced by the career of another Chicago lawyer, Adlai Stevenson II, Seith had his eye on a political career and thought the Council could be his launching pad. (In 1978, Seith, a Democrat, lost a race against Republican Senator Chuck Percy.) Seith's clash with executive director Bill Cole had led to Cole's firing, and Seith showed no signs of relinquishing his meddlesome ambition.

When I was interviewing for the job, I was aware of the Council's rich history, but also of its current problems. For one, the charter-flight loophole was likely to end soon, and with it would likely go thousands of members and a huge chunk of the budget. Alex Seith was about to step down as chairman of the board, but he'd maneuvered to retain a powerful board role. And though the new leadership of the Tribune Company had opinions more tuned than the Colonel's to the 20th century, a crusty handful of the old guard remained at the paper. The *Tribune*'s political columnist, George Tagge, characterized by Longworth as McCormick's "journalistic hatchet man,"[25] wrote several sarcastically unwelcoming articles about me and the Council on my arrival. In one, he said that the Council had stuck to its "pro-Democratic ways," and, after noting Adlai Stevenson's earlier association with the organization, Tagge wondered whether "to add Rielly to the Presidential dark horse list."[26]

Nonetheless, as I interviewed for the position and talked to Chicagoans, I realized that the Council job represented a promising opportunity. From my Ford Foundation work on the Stevenson Institute, I knew something about Chicago, and I was acquainted with several prominent citizens, including Hermon "Dutch" Smith, the former chief of Marsh & McLennan, the giant insurer, and Adlai Stevenson III, who was about to be elected a U.S. senator. What's more, as various people pointed out to me, the major businesses in Chicago—banks, manufacturers, advertisers, law firms—had been transformed recently from regional to national operations. Now the transformation was moving to the next level, to international business. As a result, the constituency of people with a serious interest in international affairs was greatly expanding.

I also admired ways in which the Chicago Council differed from its New York counterpart, which was almost the same age. The New York Council on Foreign Relations had earned a reputation for substance and produced excellent work, but it was an elite redoubt, all-male and dominated by New England WASPs and major players on Wall Street. Membership came exclusively by invitation. By contrast, the Chicago Council was open to all and welcomed women—indeed, one of its founders had been a woman, and the full-time executive director for a decade was Louise Leonard Wright.

In the end, I was happy to take the job, starting September 1, 1971. Elizabeth didn't want to move immediately to Chicago. So I rented an

---

25 *Chicago and the World*, p. 141.
26 Tagge, George, "Political Lookout," *Chicago Tribune*, June 19, 1971, p. 4.

apartment on North Lake Shore Drive, and for the first eight or nine months I commuted back and forth from Washington to Chicago. The family moved permanently to Chicago the next summer.

I started the job with one overriding goal in mind: To make the Chicago Council on Foreign Relations a full-fledged, participating member of the American foreign policy establishment, which until then had been dominated by organizations in Washington, New York, and Cambridge.

Throughout my time, the Council's headquarters consisted of offices, a large conference room, and a kitchen at 116 South Michigan Avenue, across the street from the Art Institute of Chicago. When I arrived, the staff was about 15 strong, and it averaged around 25 for most of my tenure. The budget was around $500,000, but it soon grew, and after a decade it reached around $4 million and stayed close to that level while I was there.

Even as I worked toward my goal of raising the Council's profile, I had to find a way to stabilize the organization's finances and membership rolls, both of which were going to take a severe hit when the Civil Aeronautics Board changed the rules on charter flights—likely to be soon. The flight-inflated membership still brought in considerable revenue, and while it lasted, we used the money to expand meetings and programs. We also devised ways to accommodate various constituencies. The suburban membership was dominated by women—this was at a time when many college-educated women with families were not in the workforce—so we expanded the luncheon programs that had started on the North Shore and initiated new ones in the western suburbs.

The Council had already established an elite, invitation-only subgroup within the membership—the Chicago Committee—which was patterned on the New York Council; you had to be nominated to join. It drew heavily from the city's business leadership and expanded gradually after my arrival to about 450 members. (Unfortunately, the Chicago Committee remained all-male until common sense and decency prevailed and the rule was changed in 1978.) The Chicago Committee tilted older, so we established two young leaders groups; one limited by invitation was run by James Hoge, the editor of the *Chicago Sun-Times*.

We set up a corporate service program, aimed particularly at giving briefings on international issues—often involving economics—to Chicago companies. The operation proved fruitful in increasing corporate donations to the Council. And we initiated a research program designed to attract and involve the local academic communities, especially the University of Chicago, Northwestern, Loyola, and the University of Illinois at Chicago. Eventually, that program grew to involve regional universities, such as the University of Michigan, the University of Wisconsin, the University of Illinois at Champaign-Urbana, and the University of Minnesota. Unlike the New York Council, we didn't have an in-house research arm, so we retained academics for a year or so at a time for our seminars and study groups.

The fall I arrived, the first program—planned before I was on the scene—focused on U.S.-Japanese economic relations, a subject of growing interest. Several Chicago companies—most notably Zenith—were among the most active American corporations doing business with Japan. Four young scholars of Japan from the University of Chicago provided the expertise.

All these outreach efforts paid off with a more diversified membership and financial base. The CAB rules changed, and the charter flights ended after 1976, but membership dropped by only about half, to around 12,000, far more than the Council had enjoyed before the charter program started. And even before our charter wings were clipped, we started sponsoring six or eight guided tours each year to Europe, Asia, and the Middle East. The guides were usually local academics, and we generally attracted 20 to 30 participants. Also, as the Council's reputation grew, we organized special overseas tours for board members that included programs with top foreign dignitaries, such as German Chancellor Helmut Kohl, French Foreign Minister Jean Francois-Poncet, and NATO Secretary General George Robertson.

Two programs both initiated and funded by the Ford Foundation gave major boosts to the Council's profile. I'd encountered the first while I was still at Ford. For several decades, Ford and the Carnegie Endowment for International Peace had been sponsoring conferences for government officials and other influential figures aimed at improving relations among the United States, South

America, and Europe. By the late 1960s, the conference program—entitled *Encuentro Siglo Veinto*—was withering. Participation was mixed, and many of the attendees were old.

While at Ford, I'd written a paper on political links between Western Europe and South America. Through a somewhat convoluted connection, I was asked to organize a revised Ford-Carnegie-funded conference, which was to be held in 1970 in Dorado Beach, Puerto Rico. I agreed and recruited a steering committee of 12 U.S. senators, all under 50 years of age. Senator Frank Church agreed to be co-chair. We set up some ground rules for this and future conferences. We renamed the gathering the Atlantic Conference. To establish the point that we wanted to involve the next generation of leadership, we made a rule that no one over 50 would be invited to participate. The conference would be small—no more than 50 participants. It would meet every two years, the venue rotating among Europe, North America, and South America. It would meet in November at a luxury resort someplace where the sun would likely be shining (an obvious inducement). Spouses would be welcome, but no staff—principals only. All expenses would be covered.

We decided to swing for the fences in that Dorado Beach conference: The subject would be the role of the United States in the world.

I started searching for promising participants and enlisted a strong roster, including the director of *Le Monde*; the Harvard scholar Sam Huntington; the attorney general of Canada; the deputy prime minister of Spain; Delfin Neto, the minister of finance of Brazil; and six U.S. senators, including future vice president Walter Mondale. Perhaps the most significant participant in terms of the future of the Chicago Council on Foreign Relations proved to be a young German politician named Helmut Kohl, prime minister of the province of Rhineland-Palatinate, who went on to be chancellor of Germany from 1982 to 1998.

That Dorado Beach conference turned into a big success, though not without a small crisis. I had traveled to Mainz, Germany, to invite Kohl to the conference. He was then 38 and he enthusiastically accepted. I warned him and his chief of staff that the languages of the conference were French, Spanish, and English, not German. No problem they both said—he spoke English.

Ten days before the conference opened, I got a frantic call from Kohl's chief of staff. This would be Kohl's first international conference, and he doesn't know the subject well. He absolutely needs an interpreter. I managed to find a German interpreter in Puerto Rico, and at the first formal session, she sat next to Kohl at the end of the table. For the first hour, the conversation was mostly in English, and she could translate from English to German. Then Kohl started to speak in German, and within seconds he realized that she couldn't go from German to English. Fortunately, the person seated next to Kohl was a Dutchman who spoke five languages fluently, including German, and he took over as Kohl's interpreter. Kohl's wife, Hannelore, spoke fluent English, so he had a skilled interpreter at meals and at the beach.

Kohl's positive experience at the conference led to his becoming a close friend. He visited the Council three times over the years and arranged a $3 million grant to it from the German government. During his lifetime, I often visited him on my trips to Germany. "Pay attention to people who are 45 and on the way up," my old mentor Hubert Humphrey used to exhort his staff. "They will remember it."

By the time of the next scheduled Atlantic Conference meeting in 1972, I was at the Council. The Ford Foundation and the co-chairs of the conference steering committee, including Senator Church, asked the Chicago Council on Foreign Relations to take over running the conference, and we agreed. Over the years, the Atlantic Conferences brought both the Council and Chicago to the attention of dozens of men and women who would later become high-profile world leaders. Most would remember and appreciate that when they were young and unknown, they'd been invited to meet with talented men and women who were not only stimulating but destined to govern their countries. The list included not only Kohl, but future presidents of Argentina, Chile, and Brazil, as well as scores of men and women who would go on to be foreign ministers, finance ministers, leading journalists, and celebrated professors. A young U.S. senator named Joe Biden attended an Atlantic Conference meeting in 1974 held in Taormina, Sicily.

The attention given the conferences run by a Chicago concern raised the image of the city. Chicago was no longer fly-over territory, and the success of the conferences encouraged foreign leaders to accept invitations from the Council to visit the city and appear on council programs. Thus, during my tenure, the Council featured appearances by Valery Giscard d'Estaing, Boris Yeltsin, Abba Eban, Mary Robinson, and countless others.

In June 1991, less than a year after stepping down as British prime minister, Margaret Thatcher spoke to an audience of 4,000 at the Hilton Hotel, a gathering that included a large contingent of English journalists who had flown over from London. She gave a witty nod to local passions by saying politicians should take a lesson from Michael Jordan: "How to stay aloft with no visible means of support." But she went on to proclaim her opposition to "federal Europe." Her comments made news around the world and suggested an attitude that would resound years later with Brexit.

In June 1992 when I heard that former Soviet President Mikhail Gorbachev was coming to the United States on a speaking tour, I called Dwayne Andreas, CEO of grain behemoth Archer Daniels Midland. I had become friendly with Andreas when he joined Humphrey on several trips to Europe and Asia. As co-chairman of the U.S.–Soviet Trade and Economic Council, Andreas had become an adviser to Gorbachev when he was Soviet minister of agriculture, and Andreas later became Gorbachev's closest American friend. Responding to my request, Andreas called Gorbachev, who readily agreed to come to Chicago to address the Council. En route to Chicago, Gorbachev and his wife, Raisa, stopped in Decatur, Illinois, the home of Archer Daniels Midland, and stayed overnight at the Andreas home.

Appearing the next evening at the Council dinner at the Chicago Sheraton Hotel, Gorbachev and Raisa joined a history-conscious dinner crowd of 2,500, who happily thronged the couple as they took their seats. "We have not really seen Chicago, but we have seen each other," Gorbachev told the enthusiastic audience. "We have seen each other's eyes, and I think this is more than all the sights."

Mayor Richard J. Daley never paid attention to the Council until Willy Brandt, then the chancellor of Germany, came for a visit in September 1973. Daley remembered that Brandt had formerly been mayor of West Berlin, and that got Daley's attention. He met Brandt at the airport, threw a luncheon for him at the Bismarck Hotel, and insisted on attending Brandt's lecture to the Council at the Palmer House. Daley's son, Mayor Richard M., was similarly uninterested in the Council until French President Jacques Chirac, who'd been mayor of Paris for more than a decade, appeared in February 1996. Daley met him at the airport and stayed by his side for the entire visit. The Daleys may not have been foreign policy wonks, but they clearly valued talking about how to run a city.

Though the Council's focus was foreign policy, we also drew regular visits from American politicians, particularly those with an eager eye on the White House. The presidential aspirants would usually use their appearance to articulate their views on America's role in the world. For example, in a Chicago Council speech in March 1980, Ronald Reagan said the United States and other noncommunist countries were locked in a continuous battle with "Godless communism" and its chief exporter, the Soviet Union. He argued that we should unleash a propaganda barrage to promote pride in American achievements and spread the message around the globe.

A questioner asked Governor Reagan whether, if elected president, he would bar from his cabinet a member of the Trilateral Commission, an elite leadership group founded in the 1970s to promote cooperation among Japan, Europe, and North America. (I was a member for a number of years.) In some dark corners, conspiracists have made ridiculous claims about the Commission, including that it aimed to create a world government, or, more outrageously, that it had a hand in plotting the September 11, 2001, terrorist attacks.

"No!" responded Reagan. "My good friend Caspar Weinberger is a member of the Commission. But I would not fill the top 18 positions in my cabinet with members of the Commission"—a reference to what President Jimmy Carter had done. Weinberger became secretary of defense in the Reagan administration.

Worries about the Trilateral Commission lingered throughout the decade. In 1988, in response to a question at a Chicago Council event, candidate George Herbert Walker Bush revealed that in the last six months of campaigning, the most frequently asked question was about his membership in the Trilateral Commission.

Bush's opponent, Democrat Michael Dukakis, trying to bolster his foreign policy toughness credentials and reeling from the disastrous effects of his photo op featuring a helmeted ride in an M1 Abrams tank, linked himself to Reagan's hard anti-Soviet stance. Dukakis went on to give a skeptical assessment of Mikhail Gorbachev and argued that Bush didn't understand the Soviet leader. "Mr. Gorbachev is nimble," Dukakis said.

Other presidential candidates appearing in my time included Jimmy Carter, Gary Hart, and Walter Mondale, plus a long roster of senators and current and former foreign policy officials, including Robert McNamara and Henry Kissinger.

The second program initiated by the Ford Foundation has had a more direct role in spreading the Council's name around the world. After Nixon resigned and Gerald Ford stepped into the presidency in August 1974, the foreign policy establishment worried that the country might withdraw into a new phase of isolationism. After all, Ford had little international experience, and the country was still experiencing sharp withdrawal symptoms from the debacle in Vietnam. The concern prompted a small group of Washington leaders, including Secretary of State Henry Kissinger, to travel to New York to visit the Ford Foundation. Meeting with Ford President McGeorge Bundy in September, the group asked: Would the Ford Foundation commission and finance a study of public and leadership opinion on American foreign policy? Specifically, the group wanted to know if there was continuing support for the internationalist tilt of the previous three decades or if there was a substantial danger that the U.S. would retreat into isolation. The group wanted to measure opinions of both the public at large and the country's leaders.

Ford officials agreed to underwrite the project. But who should run it? There were the usual suspects—the Brookings Institution, the New York Council on Foreign Relations, and the Carnegie Endowment for International Peace. But both Bundy and Dave Bell, Ford's international affairs vice president, knew me. Landrum Bolling, president of the Lilly Endowment, had recently spent a day visiting the Chicago Council and sent the Ford Foundation an enthusiastic report. So Ford decided to ask the Chicago Council to undertake the project. Bundy called me to outline plans for the survey and said he hoped we could publish the results early in the new year when members of Congress would be returning for the next congressional session.

The Council and I readily agreed to run the survey. I hired Louis Harris and Associates to conduct the interviews. Harris researchers interviewed 1,500 members of the public and 330 national leaders, asking 30 to 40 questions, some general (82% of the public thought economic problems required international cooperation), some quite specific (53% of the public thought the U.S. should restore diplomatic relations with Cuba). Harris completed the preliminary report in December.

Shortly before then, I got a call from my old Humphrey colleague Ted Van Dyk. He had noticed that Lou Harris, who wrote a newspaper column in those days, had scooped us and cited some of the Council findings in his column. I had to call him and threaten to sue if he repeated that.

We released the final 30-page report on March 1, 1975. The results were reassuring. To the relief of most foreign policy circles in the United States and abroad, large majorities of both the public and the leaders supported a continued active role for the U.S. in the world.

The Washington Post's David Broder wrote that "support for an active world role is virtually unchanged from what it was 20 years ago—at the height of the cold war—even though containment of communism has dropped far down as an objective of foreign policy, ranking well behind such altruistic goals as arms control, hunger relief and solving worldwide economic problems." He said the survey should encourage President Ford and other internationalists that the country was willing to participate in the world—though it remained wary of committing military forces. "What this study seems to say is that Americans have learned that the world is not ours to manage, but that they still believe the world is one."

But if Broder took considerable assurance from the findings, another *Post* columnist, Stephen S. Rosenfeld, was less sanguine. Under the headline, "The Public's Opinion: Confused," he wrote in part, "They want continued international involvement, and reduced risks, costs and cares. They want a strong United States and a smaller defense budget. They hope the United States will keep peace in the world but their taste for helping a friend under attack diminishes as the prospect of quick success falls." He added, "To be sure, diplomacy was never meant—least of all by its practitioners—to be conducted by referendum."

The survey was clearly anchored in its moment. This was the height of the oil crisis, and the public thought Saudi Arabia was the top priority country for the United States. (The Saudis were so pleased that they invited me to visit. I couldn't go, but Council Chairman Jack Gray did visit and enjoyed a royal reception.)

The leadership side of the survey drew on a carefully selected portfolio of leaders—some House and Senate members, officials in the executive branch of government, business executives, journalists, academics, religious figures, and so on. The findings exposed a considerable gap between the public and the leaders in several areas. The leaders were generally more supportive than the public of an active U.S. role in the world. For example, leaders were more supportive of possible military intervention in Western Europe (77% to 39%)—not surprising because the public would supply the fighting forces. Leaders also favored more open immigration and were more willing to embrace free trade policies.

We distributed copies of the report to news organizations, universities, think tanks, and individuals in the United States and abroad, and the findings made news worldwide. Tom Brokaw interviewed me on the *Today* show. Two of Japan's leading daily newspapers, *Asahi* and *Mainichi*, ran the results on the front page. In general, the report had special impact in Japan and Germany, the two principal losers of World War II, but also the two biggest successes of American postwar policy. A translated summary of the report was distributed to members of the Soviet Politburo by Georgi Arbatov, the top Soviet expert on America.

From its inception, the public opinion survey turned into a resounding success for the Council, bringing it useful attention while providing a valuable trove of information to the world. We repeated it every four years during my time at the Council, and it has continued, now on an annual basis, under my successors. After that first experience with Harris, we switched to the Gallup organization, and the Council remained with Gallup through my tenure at the Council.

Over the years, the principal concerns have changed, but the results have been remarkably consistent. The public has generally supported an active American role in the world while remaining wary of direct intervention. The leaders favor a somewhat more aggressive policy.

The success of the survey raises a question—theoretical in part, but one with profound practical implications: What role should the public have in formulating and implementing foreign policy? The question has deep American roots. In his farewell address, President

George Washington stated that the country's policy was "to steer clear of permanent alliances with any portion of the foreign world." (The signature phrase about avoiding "entangling alliances" came from Thomas Jefferson's inaugural address). With a few exceptions, that isolationist sentiment largely prevailed with both the government and the public for more than a century.

Breaks from isolationism started to develop in the 20th century, notably when President Woodrow Wilson campaigned for membership in the League of Nations, but the public and Congress favored holding the isolationist course. In 1940, isolationist sentiment in the United States was so pervasive that President Franklin D. Roosevelt, who had already been elected and re-elected by wide margins, had to resort to a subterfuge to lend England a few American destroyers to help avoid a defeat by Nazi Germany.

American participation in World War II ended American isolationism. With the arrival of the Cold War between the United States and the Soviet Union, a new bipartisan consensus emerged, and the Republican Party ended up supporting President Harry Truman's initiative to launch the Marshall Plan and America's participation in NATO. This shift would be sealed by the defeat of Senator Robert Taft of Ohio, leader of the isolationist wing of the Republican Party, by General Dwight Eisenhower at the Republican Convention of 1952. For most of the Cold War period, up until the height of the Vietnam War, American foreign policy would enjoy consistent bipartisan congressional support. But that still left the question of the public's role.

For the diplomat George F. Kennan, the author of the U.S. policy of containment of the Soviet Union, foreign policy should be determined by professionals like himself, people who have had training and long experience.[27] Walter Lippmann, for decades America's most influential columnist, largely shared Kennan's views.[28] Both acknowledged that the U.S. Constitution accorded a role in formulating foreign policy to Congress—in theory, representatives of public opinion. But they believed congressional participation

---
27 Kennan, George F., "The Future of Our Professional Diplomacy," *Foreign Affairs*, July 1966, pp. 566–586.

28 Walter Lippmann was one of the first to consider the role of public opinion in his book *Public Opinion*, first published in 1922.

in the foreign policy process should be limited to a small number of leaders from the Senate Foreign Relations Committee, plus the majority and minority leaders of the House and Senate, people with substantial knowledge and expertise gained through long years in leadership roles. Other members of Congress should defer to these leaders.

In the view of people like Kennan and Lippmann, the public itself was unqualified to play any significant role, as the public lacked knowledge, expertise, and experience—people rarely even paid sustained attention to foreign policy issues. What's more, Hitler's success manipulating public opinion to build national support for pernicious policies served as an ominous example.

For the two decades after World War II, when centrist policy ruled, the American public generally was willing to leave the determination of U.S. foreign policy to the executive branch of government. That started to change after 1965 with the escalation of the Vietnam War, and by March 1968 massive public opposition to the war compelled President Lyndon Johnson to modify American policy and forced Johnson to end his re-election campaign for the presidency. Both Johnson and his successor, Richard Nixon, paid intensely close attention to public sentiment (though Nixon denied it). Vietnam essentially destroyed the bipartisan consensus that had lasted for two decades and heightened attention among government leaders to the public's attitude toward international affairs.

President Jimmy Carter lost the support of much of the public over the Iran hostage crisis and lost his re-election bid. Later, President Ronald Reagan temporarily rallied support for an enlarged defense budget and heightened competition with the Soviet Union. With the arrival of Soviet President Mikhail Gorbachev and his policy of Glasnost, a new temporary consensus obtained both in Congress and in the country.

Public support for military participation in wars in Iraq and Afghanistan, though strong at first, would never regain the level of support of the Cold War period, and eventually both actions drew wide opposition. At the same time, the surveys have shown a strong inclination among the public to support humanitarian aid and protect human rights, while the leaders surveyed are much less enthusiastic on these points. Perhaps in part because of the strong public support for humanitarian issues, President Joe Biden was able to rally public backing for substantial financial support for Ukraine after the Russian attack in 2022. As of this writing, neo-isolationist criticism of U.S. efforts on behalf of Ukraine—warily iterated by former President Donald Trump and Florida Governor Ron DeSantis—has largely failed to gain traction with the public.

An American president has wide discretion in foreign policy and ultimately—with some degree of input from Congress—has the power to act. But a wise chief executive stays alert to the attitude of the public. Historically, that has often meant selling an initiative to the media. As the Vietnam War was heating up, the Johnson administration conducted an ambitious "courtship of Walter Lippmann," as historian Fredrik Logevall puts it[29]—including at least one long meeting with President Johnson himself— unsuccessfully trying to change Lippmann's opposition to American military involvement. In any case, the media is an imperfect messenger because it easily focuses on issues that are marginal but grab attention—the taking of a hostage, for example. And in the last two decades, with the rise of the internet, the media landscape has become far more complex and harder to influence. Almost anyone can capture attention with a bold statement, even if untrue.

In short, the public opinion surveys run by the Chicago Council provide a useful tool for decision-makers, but Kennan and Lippmann had this much right: Public opinion is rarely a substitute for the knowledgeable advice of experts in the field.

Early on in my tenure at the Council, a publishing opportunity came to us through Sam Huntington at Harvard. While pursuing his PhD, he became a close friend of another PhD student, Warren Manshel. Huntington went on to acclaim as a scholar of international relations, while Manshel made a fortune on Wall Street. In the late 1960s, the two divided over Vietnam—Huntington for a time largely supporting Johnson's policy and Manshel strongly opposing it. The two decided to found a new quarterly journal, *Foreign Policy*, in which conflicting points of view on Vietnam and other subjects could be aired.

---

29 Logevall, Fredrik, "First Among Critics: Walter Lippmann and the Vietnam War," *The Journal of American-East Asian Relations*, Winter 1995, pp. 351-375.

Foreign Affairs, the publication put out by the New York Council on Foreign Relations, had become the most important foreign policy journal in the world, but it had correctly come to be seen as the voice of the establishment, frequently running articles that explained the vision of the current administration. Huntington and Manshel wanted to create a more independent journal, one that wouldn't hesitate to publish articles critical of current U.S. policy. Manshel provided the funding, and the first issue came out in late 1970. Arguments about Vietnam dominated the early issues.

Not long after I moved to Chicago, Huntington called me and asked if the Council would have an interest in associating with the new publication. We worked out an arrangement whereby Council benefactors would get complimentary subscriptions, thus helping *Foreign Policy* build subscribers in the Midwest. In return, I would join the editorial board and the magazine would give special consideration to publishing Council-generated articles.

At around the same time, the Carnegie Endowment for International Peace, under my old friend Tom Hughes, its new president, agreed to assume full financial and editorial responsibility for the publication. Hughes became chairman of *Foreign Policy*'s editorial board. Soon Richard Holbrooke took over as managing editor on his way to a notable diplomatic career.

The Council's relationship with *Foreign Policy* has proved decidedly fruitful. Holbrooke hosted a press conference in Washington to introduce the first public opinion report. The magazine published my first article on the findings in its second issue and five more articles in the ensuing years. Many other papers that came out of Council research, seminars, and the Atlantic Conference also appeared in the pages of *Foreign Policy*. I remained on the board through three decades.

For a decade or so, the editorial board met twice a year in Warren Manshel's Fifth Avenue apartment, followed by a six-course gourmet dinner. Even as the Vietnam War was winding down, arguments about Vietnam policy dominated the early meetings, and the debates often grew fiery. Huntington and board member Zbigniew Brzezinski had helped draft Humphrey's campaign statement against the war, but both had been early supporters and remained strong anti-communists. Another board member, Yale professor Richard Cooper, still supported an American military presence. At one meeting, Cooper's comments so provoked *Foreign Policy* board member David Halberstam that he stood up and shouted, "I won't remain in the same room with warmongers." He left immediately and disappeared from the board. But regardless of how acrimonious the discussion became, afterward we always sat down for a genial and delicious dinner.

For my first decade at the Council, the Ford Foundation was the largest funder of the organization. At the time, the only substantial foundation in Chicago was the Chicago Community Trust. When I asked its director, Bruce Newman, about possible funding for the Council, he said the Trust only supported local projects and had no interest in the Council. That would change, but it took years.

The foundation landscape improved dramatically starting in the early 1980s when the John D. and Catherine T. MacArthur Foundation came on stream. Founded by the rich, eccentric insurance mogul John MacArthur, the MacArthur Foundation, based in Chicago, became the largest foundation funder of the public opinion surveys. That arrangement changed with the arrival of Adele Simmons as president of the foundation in 1989. The daughter of Dutch Smith, a former Council chairman, Simmons had been a dean at Princeton and president of Hampshire College. For reasons that I never fully grasped and that seemed to be rooted in a misunderstanding several years before with Ruth Adams, head of MacArthur's international division, the foundation substantially reduced a scheduled donation and for a time cut off funding entirely. Happily, the contributions returned when a new foundation president arrived in 1999.

Meantime, however, other foundations stepped up their support through the 1980s and 1990s. Helmut Kohl, a strong supporter of the Council, arranged contributions from major German sources, including the Thyssen, Krupp, and Volkswagen Foundations. In all, 20 foundations from around the world gave grants to the Council, as did eight foundations in the United States. Council Vice President and Program Director Arthur Cyr contributed significantly to the success in securing foundation funding, especially through his extensive contacts in Asia. The generous support from foundations helped build a budget surplus every year for 30 years, and that enabled the Council to accumulate a reserve of over $6,000,000. It had been around $50,000 when I arrived. In all, the Council received 30 foundation grants during my tenure.

My frugal management also helped produce the reserve, but in retrospect, I realize I went too far. My experience at Ford overseeing nonprofits, particularly the Adlai Stevenson Institute, had taught me that these organizations were often sloppy with their money and given to needless overspending. I wanted to make sure the Council stayed lean. As a result, I never hired a strong development team to raise funds—most of the fundraising was done by me and by Art Cyr with an occasional assist by a board member. A mistake. With a high-powered development director, the Council certainly could have raised more money and hence expanded its programs.

My work on the council brought many new friendships and solidified others, one of the most substantial being with Helmut Kohl. Our friendship extended over four decades and included regular meetings in Bonn, Berlin, Chicago, New York, and Washington. Kohl was not fluent in English and encouraged me to bolster my German, which I had neglected after passing the German language requirement for my PhD. So I enrolled twice in German language programs at the Goethe-Institut in Germany and engaged a private tutor in Chicago for four years. Eventually, Kohl and I conversed easily in German.

Over the decades, I came to know members of his family. When his son Walter enrolled at Harvard, my daughter Catherine, who was at the Kennedy School, gave a reception to introduce him. When Kohl's wife Hannelore received an award from the United Service Organization for her years of attentiveness to American soldiers in Germany, I flew to Washington to welcome her.

Kohl was a brilliant, serious man, but he enjoyed gossip. Once, in the early 1990s, when he was still chancellor, he heard that I would be in Berlin and invited me to spend a Saturday morning with him at his Berlin retreat. For over two hours, he regaled me with unvarnished comments about the wives of world leaders he knew. Barbara Bush was a reassuring and positive influence on President George Herbert Walker Bush. In contrast, Nancy Reagan was a prima donna who provoked her husband's worst reactions. Boris Yeltsin's wife was a calming influence on her husband, including when he was drinking. Raisa Gorbachev, like Nancy Reagan, sought the limelight and was always competing with her husband.

At that point, Kohl had met Hillary Clinton only briefly, and he grilled me at length about her. I couldn't be of much help. Though I once had a long conversation with her in Davos at the World Economic Forum, I did not know her well. Kohl was hoping I could assure him that Hillary Clinton was not like Nancy Reagan and Raisa Gorbachev—by his reading, dark influences on their husbands.

Several years after retiring from the Council, I spent a month at the American Academy in Berlin on a fellowship. Kohl was by now the former chancellor and a widower; his wife Hannelore had died two years before. He invited my wife, Irene, and me for dinner, and we met his future wife, an attractive 38-year-old named Maike Richter. We saw him again in 2016 later at his private home in Ludwigshafen. By then, he had suffered the second of two falls, which left him confined to a wheelchair with his speech gravely impaired. We were shocked to see how diminished he was—frail and barely able to speak. During a five-hour visit, Maike (now Maike Kohl-Richter) deciphered Kohl's greatly impaired speech during a subdued but wide-ranging conversation. He died a year later.

In 1972, shortly after my arrival at the Council, the organization celebrated its 50th anniversary with a gala dinner. The event is memorable today because it marked a rapprochement with our old adversary, the *Tribune*. By then, Colonel McCormick's acolytes had largely left the paper, and the new leadership recognized the value of global interests. At a Council meeting that year, the *Tribune* editor, Clayton Kirkpatrick, spoke eloquently of the importance of foreign news, and the paper bought a table at the anniversary dinner.

Twenty-five years later, the Council's 75th anniversary celebration featured a speech by Helmut Kohl, then in his 15th year as German chancellor. Unlike Margaret Thatcher at her appearance in 1991, he spoke glowingly of the European Union, though he said, "once Europeans have found their place in this European house, they will keep one room open on a permanent lease for the Americans." He went on to praise the Council for "its tremendous importance in building bridges from America and from Chicago to the rest of the world."

The *Tribune*'s long report on the anniversary banquet at the Hilton Hotel spoke of the civic role of the Council and described Chicagoans as being "proud as punch to be home to such a world-renowned fixture." By then, Colonel McCormick's philanthropic legacy, the McCormick Foundation, was a regular contributor to the Council.

The Council's success came in great part from the inspired leadership of members of the board of directors, as well as from the talent and dedication of long time Council staffers. With these and the many more council leaders over our shared 30 years, I found that what transformed our relationships into friendships was a strong sense of common mission and an insatiable work ethic, informed by high intelligence and human decency.

Council Chairman Jack Gray of Hart Schaffner Marx played a decisive role in the early years in securing the support of the corporate community. Chairman John Bryan, CEO of Sara Lee and dean of the Chicago business/civic establishment, connected the Council with world leaders such as Margaret Thatcher and with the World Economic Forum in Davos. Lawyers Edmund Stephan of the firm then known as Mayer Brown & Platt and Jeff Shields of Garner Carton & Douglas provided wise counsel to me over three decades. Civic leaders and philanthropists Shirley Welsh Ryan and John Manley were among the Council's most generous supporters, which included their funding the Council's multifaceted program for young people. Under my successor, Marshall Bouton, Manley hosted the annual fundraising dinner for almost two decades, making him one of the largest benefactors in the Council's history. In addition to his many equally generous gifts, Manley always employed his impressive strategic skills to maximize the benefit to the council.

Vice President and Program Director Arthur Cyr provided strong leadership in building the Council's diverse program as well as in foundation fundraising. Multilingual program officer Lotti Ross played an indispensable role in the success of the Atlantic Conference. Vice President of Finance Robert Cordes played a critical role in achieving a budget surplus over a period of three decades.

Around the time of the anniversary banquet, I started thinking about my departure from the Council. The organization was financially solid, and I had accomplished my chief goal: to make the Council a voice in the American foreign policy establishment.

We'd launched a groundbreaking survey and created countless important programs. Leaders from around the world had spoken to our audiences. I had been approached about returning to academia, and I was growing eager to travel on my own time. At the initiative of Council Chairman John Bryan, I arranged with the executive committee to set a retirement date of September 1, 2001, exactly 30 years after the day I started.

As the date neared, I gave a talk at the University Club, discussing what I called the same key question that was raised when the Chicago Council on Foreign Relations was founded in 1922: the role of the United States in the world. Since that early isolationist era, the country had emerged as a hegemonic power, and I pointed out the dangers lurking when the U.S. is unchallenged. Already, domestic politics were driving American foreign policy, and the country's diplomacy reflected an arrogance that easily bred resentment. I chided Congress for spending heavily on military budgets while cutting dramatically in foreign aid. At the same time, I applauded Chicago for a growing international role, led particularly by savvy businesses and organizations working internationally. As a marker of how times had changed, the *Chicago Tribune* reprinted the speech in its entirety.

The Council selected Marshall Bouton, an Asia and India expert and deputy director of the Asia Society, as my successor. My old friend George Robertson, the secretary general of NATO, came to bid my farewell at a special meeting. The Council organized a banquet, featuring a keynote by former Secretary of State James Baker. As planned, I left on September 1, 2001, and 10 days later the world of foreign policy took yet another dark turn.

CHAPTER 13
UPHEAVAL AT HOME

My move to Chicago to take the job with the Chicago Council on Foreign Relations opened a period of upheaval in the life of my family. Having friendship as the prime value in my life since childhood, it was during this period that it took on even greater meaning for me.

After I had been commuting on weekends between Chicago and Washington for 10 months, Elizabeth decided she was prepared to move to Chicago. We sold the house on Rittenhouse Street in Chevy Chase and moved in mid-August 1972 to a rented modern house in the North Shore suburb of Kenilworth, which lies between Wilmette and Winnetka. Because Elizabeth's sister and brother-in-law, Peggy and Jack Bird, lived in Winnetka, we were generally familiar with the area.

Our children seemed happy with the move to suburban Chicago, and they were pleased to have the family reunited. Our oldest daughter, Mary Ellen, then 13, enrolled at Sears public school in Kenilworth. Cathy, 12, and the younger boys, Tom, 8, and John, 7, went to Saints Faith, Hope and Charity parochial school in nearby Winnetka. Tom later enrolled at Harper public school in Wilmette.

Elizabeth remained unhappy in the marriage. Early Christmas morning, she quietly disappeared from the house. I didn't have a satisfactory explanation for the children, and, naturally, they were deeply upset. Later that day, I received a message that she was filing for a temporary separation. This was all a huge shock and enormously alarming.

I realize now that in my pain and trauma I was too reticent with the children and didn't speak to them with enough candor about what was going on. Children need to hear the truth.

"I remember asking over and over again, 'Where's Mom? When is she coming back?' and never getting a straight answer," recalled John, who was eight at the time. "That was very difficult."

"It was very traumatic, mainly because we did not know what was going on," said Mary Ellen, who had just turned 14. "The lack of communication to us as kids added to the stress and sadness of the situation."-

I strongly disagreed with Elizabeth's decision to separate, but I always remained appreciative of her role in bringing four attractive children into the world and was determined to do anything to build strong and positive mother–child relationships. The divorce was finalized at the end of 1973. (The Catholic Church later formally annulled the marriage, which gave me permission to remarry in the Church.)

With four young children at home, I needed qualified help. I advertised for a housekeeper in the archdiocese newspaper and quickly hired Sister Celine Hynes, a lively 62-year-old who had been principal of St. Malachy School but had retired early. She moved in with us and proved to be indispensable, soon developing a warm relationship with all four children.

"Sister Celine was like a smart, loving grandmotherly figure, and I absolutely loved her and needed her," Tom told me years later. "She knew everyone was in such acute pain, including you, that she was pretty good at making people feel better."

Cathy, who was into her teens and entering high school, remembered that Sister Celine was a good influence on the boys, who were considerably younger. She organized the house efficiently—going so far as to write out menus. And she was practical. "She only wore her habit when she went to the jeweler because she would get a discount."

We had been in Kenilworth in a rented house for just a year when the village held a referendum on whether to build a single public tennis court. Residents overwhelmingly voted it down—many of them or their neighbors had their own, private courts. That signaled to me that Kenilworth would never provide the sorts of services suitable to raising four kids. So I bought a four-bedroom, half-century-old Tudor house six blocks away in the Kenilworth Gardens neighborhood of Wilmette, a town with excellent public facilities, including a good library, a beautiful beach, an athletic center, and strong schools. That turned out to be a fine place to raise children.

Sister Celine stayed with us for four and a half years, which included an extended summer stay at the Aspen Institute for Humanistic Studies in Colorado, where I participated in a seminar, and a summer in Cambridge while I was a visiting scholar at the Harvard Center for International Affairs. As the kids grew more independent, Sister Celine left to lead a more restful life, but she stayed in touch with them for years, becoming a close friend and advisor to Irene, my second wife. Later on, I hired graduate students from Northwestern University in nearby Evanston to live with us and lend a hand.

All four children went on to graduate from Winnetka's New Trier High School and go on to college and graduate-school experiences at a variety of schools, including Stanford, Georgetown, Yale, and Harvard. Tom and John did not finish college but have gone on to productive careers.

Elizabeth took a position as special assistant to an officer of the American Bar Association, which was headquartered in Chicago, and she worked there for 25 years before retiring. At that point, she moved to Arizona. I've had little contact with her in recent decades, but the children have continued to see her.

In 1974 I met a young woman, Henrietta Pons, who came from a prominent Czech-American family in Riverside, Illinois. She had graduated from Stanford and the Columbia University School of International Affairs and was working in the publishing field. She lived 10 blocks away in Winnetka. We soon became a couple and were together for seven years, traveling at times to Jamaica, Paris, and Prague, where she had relatives.

Although we had a close relationship, we never in seven years discussed marriage—we both understood implicitly that it wouldn't work. I was a single man with responsibility for raising four children.

She was an accomplished professional and financially independent woman. In 1981 we parted ways, and it was painful on both sides. But it was the right decision. I wanted to marry again, but I concluded that was unlikely while I still had such heavy family responsibilities. I will always have a fond memory of Henrietta. She brought joy into my life at a difficult time.

These first few years were the most challenging for all of us, and since I never did develop skill at mothering, I worked hard to draw on resources to give all I could to the children. And the greatest resource I had was my array of friends. The friendships I developed around the world over a period of two decades enabled me to bring my children to the world and the world to them.

While studying in England, Mary Ellen formed a friendship with my longtime friend Tom McNally, a member of Parliament and then the chief of staff to Prime Minister Jim Callahan. Cathy developed a close relationship with the Piero and Carla Bassetti family in Milan and the Tom and Hanneke Kerstein family in the Netherlands. Piero, former governor of Lombardy, served with me on the Trilateral Commission. Tom Kerstein and I were friends since the early 1960s days of our association with the Christian Democrats of Europe.

In Paris, Tom Rielly became a close friend of Paul and Mary Anderson and Judith Symonds. Paul Anderson represented Booz Allen Hamilton, and Judith was a consultant and professor at Sciences Po. They fed him, housed him, and loved him during his student days at the Sorbonne. John began joining me on the Council ski trips as soon as he could and built lasting friendships with Dr. John Hutcherson, a champion skier from Denver, and others.

All of these people were highly educated and cosmopolitan, with broad interests in art, education, culture, and foreign policy. While these friendships may have begun as official contacts and introductions, they were not transactional as is so often true in present times. They were built on shared interests, shared values, shared purposes, and often a common culture. The friendships are many decades old and still going strong, for which I will always be deeply thankful.

By September 1985, the kids were largely out of the house, either in college or in post-college jobs. That month, at a symposium of the Chicago Council on Foreign Relations at the Michigan Shores Club in Wilmette, I met Irene Diedrich, principal of an elementary school in Glenview. She was beautiful, intelligent, charming, Catholic, and eligible. Irene had grown up in Wauconda, Illinois, a lakeside community 40 miles north of Chicago. Her father was a milkman in Chicago, her mother an office worker, and the family with four children struggled financially. She attended Loyola University at night while working full time and earned a BA after eight years. She later taught and served as principal at several schools, at one point taking a year off to finish a doctorate in school leadership at the University of Illinois at Urbana-Champaign. After retiring as assistant superintendent of Glenview Public Schools District 34, she worked for 12 years for the North Cook Intermediate Service Center as a consultant, developing and organizing seminars for school administrators. She also taught courses in school leadership as an adjunct at the University of Illinois and took on various short-term consulting projects.

Two years after Irene and I met, we married. It was the best decision I ever made. For 36 years she has brought joy into my life and into the lives of my family and friends.

After I retired from the Chicago Council on Foreign Relations, I took teaching jobs at Northwestern University and the Graduate School of International Relations and Pacific Affairs at the University of California, San Diego. At both schools, I taught a seminar on American foreign policy from President Kennedy to the present. I enjoyed teaching, and for almost two decades we divided life between Northwestern in the fall and San Diego during the winter.

Home life got even better. In 2002, we were invited by friends to join an apartment co-op in Paris. Since then, we have spent two months a year in Paris, always residing in the Sixth Arrondissement near the Jardin du Luxembourg. In 2018, I was invited to become a visiting fellow at Clare Hall, one of the graduate colleges of Cambridge University in England. Following a two-year pandemic interval, we now divide our time between two months in the spring in Cambridge and two months in the autumn in Paris.

Happily, my kids have all done well. After graduating from Stanford, Mary Ellen took a job at Oracle, which after a few years sent her to Sydney, Australia, to run the company's telemarketing operation there. In Australia, she met a Scotsman, and they married and had a daughter, Fiona, though they eventually divorced. Mary Ellen later worked for the News Corporation and now is the director of special gifts at the University of Sydney. Her daughter, Fiona Elizabeth Rielly Noble, holds a double BA/BFA degree from the University of New South Wales as well as a master of social work, and she is a therapeutic case manager at Family Spirit, an NGO serving children who have been removed from family.

Cathy also graduated from Stanford, then earned a master's in political economy at Harvard. She won a Fulbright to Cameroon, where she explored how that country built a strong agricultural base. Later, she turned her work there into a PhD at the Kennedy School at Harvard. After some years of teaching and international consulting, she now runs an NGO, Rubia, focusing on women's issues in Afghanistan and in Africa. Her husband, James Hellinger, is a physician who has specialized in AIDS research and treatment. They have a son, Jason, in business and a daughter, Riley, who just earned a BA at Berkeley and is now a social worker focusing on violence prevention.

I never anticipated being a grandfather, nor imagined the immense joy that special role has brought. I'm blessed with three beautiful, talented contributors to society, and I don't have the worries of being a parent.

Tom attended Georgetown, Yale, and the Sorbonne before moving to California, where he worked on several start-up technology companies and founded PlanetOut, an online social media company for the LGBTQ community. He is a gifted stand-up comic, and after performing at TED events for a few years, he joined the nonprofit and ran several TED programs out of the organization's headquarters in New York. Now he lives near Palm Springs and represents TED on the West Coast.

John attended my old school, St. John's University, but left after two years to move to Telluride, Colorado, where he followed his conviction that the most important thing in life was to ski 100 days a year. Later, he worked in hospitality and earned a sommelier license, and over the next several decades served as a high-end salesman for major wine companies. Recently, he returned to Telluride, still connected to the wine business.

I am in regular contact with my surviving siblings. My sister, Mary, after combining a career as a medical librarian with raising seven children, continues to be active at 94 in Minnesota. My brother Jim, after a long teaching career in high schools in Michigan, is now retired, and with his wife, Suzanne, lives in suburban Chicago near their two daughters and their families. My brother Bernard, after a long career as a small businessman in Dover, New Hampshire, is now retired and living in a local retirement home.

When I turned 90 in December 2022, all my children came to Wilmette for a celebration. They joined my two siblings still able to travel, my many nieces and nephews and dozens of friends at a festive dinner. Tom choreographed and led the evening's presentations. He put his comic gifts to work affectionately, talking about me and the family, and Mary Ellen, Cathy, and John also spoke warmly. Irene has arranged similar parties each decade since I turned 60. Though the number of friends has declined over the decades as age has taken its toll, we still had a good turnout for my 90th. As I move into my tenth decade, it's particularly gratifying to see my children leading interesting and fulfilling lives.

CHAPTER 14

LOOKING BACK– AND AHEAD

I have been involved with American foreign policy from the high mark of U.S. hegemony in the 1960s to the years of decline following the debacle of the Vietnam War and later failures in Iraq and Afghanistan. I began teaching a seminar on American foreign policy in the government department at Harvard University in January 1961, a few days before President-elect John F. Kennedy was inaugurated. President Kennedy's claim in his inaugural address that the United States "would pay any price, bear any burden" to protect liberty around the world reflected the pervasive optimism in American society at the time. Within months, that confidence in American action led to the hubris manifested in the Bay of Pigs fiasco in Cuba. A year later, resolution combined with restraint produced a decisive shift in the East–West balance of power as President Kennedy forced Soviet Premier Nikita Khrushchev to abandon his plans to install offensive missiles in Cuba. A year later would see the first significant arms-control agreement between the United States and the Soviet Union, along with new trade agreements. Although the United States–Soviet competition dominated the first two years of the Kennedy administration, Kennedy's favorite foreign policy initiative, the Alliance for Progress, launched in early 1961, was designed to fundamentally transform U.S. relations with Latin America.

In its use of economic and technical support, the Alliance echoed the Marshall Plan, which itself represented a high point of the foreign policy practice that came to be known as liberal internationalism. That's an approach that features a faith in cooperation among nations, a rejection of authoritarianism, a belief in protecting human rights, and a commitment to favoring democratic governments.

Liberal internationalism is fundamentally less confrontational than the other pole of postwar American diplomacy, the policy of realism (or its more pejorative twin, realpolitik). That policy features a recognition that nations operate in their own interests and that power comes in various forms, and to be effective you must be prepared, depending on the circumstances, to deal with nondemocratic nations.

In practice, the two policies were often combined. Most American foreign policy leaders in the postwar decades believed in liberal internationalism, but they qualified it with an element of realism. (The re-election of Donald Trump seriously disrupts this tradition, as I will discuss more fully later.) The combination was true particularly of the six men lionized in the excellent book *The Wise Men*,[30] by Evan Thomas and Walter Isaacson: George Kennan, John McCloy, Charles Bohlen, Averell Harriman, Dean Acheson, and Robert Lovett. Their liberal internationalism tilted toward realism when the overriding concern was opposing the Soviet Union, the basis of the Cold War. Hence a succession of administrations had dealings with the dictators Francisco Franco in Spain and Antonio Salazar in Portugal because preventing the expansion of Soviet influence in Europe was the controlling motive.

Similarly, George Kennan's influential containment policy, which dominated American Cold War thinking, was essentially a realist approach. In his famous cable, later turned into an article published in 1947 in *Foreign Affairs*[31] and signed "X," he argued that the United States should vigorously oppose Soviet expansion, "containing" the spread of communism. But Kennan was focusing primarily on Europe. To his dismay, American leaders broadened the concept

---

30 Isaacson, Walter, and Evan Thomas, *The Wise Men*, Simon & Schuster (1986).
31 "X" (George F. Kennan), "The Sources of Soviet Conduct," *Foreign Affairs*, July 1947.

worldwide into the so-called Truman Doctrine, a vow to lend support, including military support, to any democratic government threatened by communist forces.

American diplomacy weathered the first decades of the Cold War with relative success, yet it's possible to draw a line from the Truman Doctrine to Kennedy's "any price, any burden" into the terribly misguided American intervention in Vietnam—and even beyond that to military interventions in Iraq and Afghanistan.

When Richard Nixon entered the White House in January 1969, the driving force in American foreign policy moved more toward realism than liberal internationalism. Both Nixon and his national security adviser, Henry Kissinger, thought liberal internationalism was too idealistic and naïve. In their view, you deal with what's there, even if the government is harshly authoritarian. Nixon and Kissinger immediately sought to end the diplomatic isolation of communist China and began a series of measures that eventually reopened diplomatic relations between the U.S. and China. At the same time, Nixon began measures to reach a diplomatic détente with the Kremlin, which led to a substantial arms-control agreement between the United States and the Soviet Union.

With Jimmy Carter's defeat of Gerald Ford in the presidential election of 1976, the Nixon-Kissinger policy of realism was largely revoked, at least, at first. President Carter announced his priority for defending human rights, especially against authoritarian dictators of either the right or the left. Still, the 1978 Camp David Accords, which outlined a route to peace between Egypt and Israel, drew on both realism and liberal internationalism.

Ronald Reagan's election in November 1980 swung the emphasis back to realism. Reagan became widely known for his sympathy for dictators such as Ferdinand Marcos in the Philippines and Augusto Pinochet in Chile. Reagan's secretary of state, George Shultz, carried some strains of liberal internationalism, and he eventually persuaded Reagan to pressure Pinochet to honor his commitment to step down after his defeat in a 1988 referendum, known as the plebiscite. Also, under pressure from Secretary Shultz, Reagan acknowledged that Soviet leader Mikhail Gorbachev represented a significant change of Soviet policy, and Reagan eventually signed several arms-control agreements with the new Soviet government.

Reagan's successor, President George Herbert Walker Bush, continued the policy of reconciliation with Russia and presided over the peaceful unification of Germany. Though Bush led a coalition of countries into the Gulf War in 1990 after Iraq invaded Kuwait, when the Bosnian Civil War broke out in 1992, Secretary of State James Baker declared that "we don't have a dog in that fight," and the Bush administration declined to get involved. The election of Bill Clinton led to a reversal of this policy, and the United States led a coalition of NATO countries that intervened in the Bosnian war.

With the shocking attacks by Islamic terrorists on New York and the Pentagon on September 11, 2001, President George W. Bush led the United States into a "war on terror," including a military retaliation against the Taliban government in Afghanistan and later the invasion of Iraq to oust President Saddam Hussein. The militant response to 9/11 falls outside the liberal internationalism/realist axis that had dominated postwar policy. The country's leadership was distracted from other global concerns—China's rising influence, for example— and the results of the American interventions were at best extremely uneven. Bush's successor, Barack Obama, declaring Iraq "to be the wrong war," proceeded to send additional troops to Afghanistan, where American-led Western forces were thwarted, eventually leading to an embarrassing withdrawal by the Biden administration.

Less than a year later, however, Biden showed the United States could still command leadership in the world by creating a powerful coalition of nations to oppose the Russian invasion of Ukraine. Though supplying extensive military aid to Ukraine, the United States has determinedly avoided a military commitment of its own.

Although the United States has never fully recovered from the defeat in Vietnam, the U.S. has remained a global power in the decades that followed. However, the American invasions of Iraq and Afghanistan haven't come close to achieving the clear victory that the United States won over the Soviet Union during the Cold War. Indeed, it is increasingly hard to deny that the U.S. interventions in Iraq and Afghanistan represent defeats.

Will more misguided interventions follow? That question raises an obvious corollary: Why didn't U.S. leadership learn more from the Vietnam fiasco? Why did the government continue to wade into conflicts in far-flung venues with cultures and political traditions far different from those in the United States?

The answer, I suspect, goes to a combination of hubris and good intentions, however misguided. We remain the most powerful country in the world, with a massive military force—the Pentagon budget is by far the largest in the world. For policymakers, it's hard to grasp that that kind of might can't always dominate. What's more, the power at America's disposal recalls that old adage: When you're holding a hammer, everything looks like a nail. Even after Vietnam, a lot of people with a voice in government think we should use the country's military might to impose our will on the rest of the world. And many of them believe that it's within the country's power to transform distant, alien cultures. They forget or reject the fact that Vietnam taught the impossibility of achieving that.

Like so many others, I failed to oppose the commitment of U.S. military forces to combat terrorism in the Middle East. Like others, I have been slow to recognize the limits of American power—in particular, I refer to the limits of American attempts, through a combination of wealth, technology, and military force, to successfully transform remote cultures into democratic societies whose values would eventually parallel our own. Believing our conduct to be virtuous, we have too often indulged in what the French philosopher Henry Dumery called "la tentation de faire du bien" (the temptation to do good), not only to insist that virtue be done, but our particular version of virtue in our particular way.[32] When it comes to Vietnam, Iraq, and Afghanistan, societies totally different in culture from American and European societies, we have largely failed.

The course of events since Vietnam has clarified for me the limits of American interventions abroad. I can only hope our current and future leaders have absorbed the same lessons. Unfortunately, some Republicans, following the lead of Donald Trump, have drawn the wrong lesson—for example, opposing the Biden administration's robust support for Ukraine in resisting Russia's unprovoked attack. Some, including Trump's second-term vice president, JD Vance, are actively seeking a return to the isolationist policies that proved so disastrous after World War I.

My years in Washington gave me a vivid picture of how leadership

---

[32] Dumery, Henry, "La tentation de faire du bien," *Esprit*, January, 1955.

can affect policy. Whether the policy being followed is liberal internationalism or realism, the quality of leadership proves decisively important. In World War II, the allied victory was due in great part to the leadership of Roosevelt, Churchill, and Stalin. The revival of the Western world after the war was led by Truman, Eisenhower, U.K. Prime Minister Clement Atlee, German Chancellor Konrad Adenauer, and French President Charles de Gaulle. The late Cold War period featured Reagan, German Chancellor Helmut Kohl, and Soviet President Mikhail Gorbachev.

The two leaders who had the greatest direct impact on my life were John F. Kennedy and Hubert Humphrey. Though they shared many views—particularly on foreign policy—they had strikingly different backgrounds and personalities, and I think that difference influenced the decisions they made or might have made. I've already described Humphrey's hardscrabble Midwestern youth. Later, as mayor of Minneapolis and long-serving senator, Humphrey was admired for his intelligence, vision, perseverance, and personal warmth. His humanitarian instincts were widely recognized, as was his sympathy for the poor and disadvantaged. He always argued that in public service, priority should be given to those "at the beginning of life and those at the end of life." A man of passionate convictions, he nonetheless befriended and respected people whose views he did not share. Although he never publicly traded on his religious affiliation, he practiced the Christian virtues of generosity, modesty, and tolerance.

But practicing the Christian virtues is not always the surest recipe for political success, and those virtues don't necessarily provide the backbone to make difficult decisions. As vice president, Hubert Humphrey didn't have the confidence to stand up to Lyndon Johnson's bullying and intimidation. At the same time, Humphrey found JFK's New Frontiersmen, such as Robert McNamara and McGeorge Bundy, a bit threatening. Hence, against his better instincts, Humphrey slipped into a wholehearted embrace of Johnson's escalation of the Vietnam War.

In contrast, John Kennedy was fully at ease with brilliant, accomplished people. I recall hearing of an argument between Kennedy and Bundy that went on all day. Kennedy grew up in a privileged family. He was a Harvard grad and a war hero. Early in his political career, he learned to stand up to an imposing and demanding father. Kennedy was not more gifted intellectually than Humphrey, but his life experience prior to the presidency had instilled great self-confidence. That self-confidence did not prevent his acquiescence in the Bay of Pigs disaster in Cuba in 1961. But it did help him resist the pressure from McNamara and the Joint Chiefs of Staff to send combat troops to Vietnam.

We will never know how he would have proceeded on Vietnam if he had lived and been re-elected in 1964. The debate continues. But during Kennedy's time in office, the American troops in Vietnam were advisory only. Kennedy told associates on a number of occasions that he thought the United States was overcommitted in Southeast Asia. He hinted that if he were re-elected, he would withdraw from Vietnam. It is true that he had appointed McNamara, Bundy, and Rusk, all key architects of the war. But as Gordon M. Goldstein titled a chapter in his slender 2008 volume, *Lessons in Disaster: McGeorge Bundy and the Path to War in Vietnam*,[33] "Counselors Advise But Presidents Decide."

On repeated occasions, McNamara and the Joint Chiefs of Staff advised President Kennedy to send combat troops to Vietnam. Kennedy repeatedly said no. McNamara and the Joint Chiefs repeatedly gave the same advice to President Johnson. He repeatedly said yes. By March 1968 when Johnson announced that he would not run again, there were 540,000 U.S. combat troops in Vietnam. On November 22, 1963, when Kennedy was shot, there were none. President Johnson did more for poor people in the United States than any president other than FDR. But it was Lyndon Baines Johnson's decisions that led to the greatest military disaster in American history.

With the end of the Vietnam War and through the breakup of the Soviet Union, economic concerns have played a greater role in America's foreign policy. This is reflected most vividly in oil policy, as the United States has taken a strongly realist turn in dealing with the Middle East oil states. Arguably, the Gulf War in the early 1990s had much to do with maintaining the flow of oil to the West.

While oil remains a formidable driver of American foreign policy,

---

[33] Goldstein, Gordon M., *Lessons in Disaster: McGeorge Bundy and the Path to War in Vietnam*, Times Books (2008).

another product has recently grown in influence. Tom Friedman put it well in a recent *New York Times* column: "As more and more products and services became digitized and electrified, the microchips that powered everything became the new oil."[34] The implications are profound, not least because Taiwan is a key manufacturer of microchips.

Another economic issue—the reduction of trade barriers—has been less contentious, at least until recently. Though the term "globalization" has been around for more than a century, I don't recall ever hearing it during my time in Washington. But by the 1990s, the word had become a favorite, and globalization was spreading technology and breaking down trade restrictions across the world. For the most part, both major American political parties supported globalization, and in many respects, this has turned out well. For example, the advantages have outweighed the negatives with the North American Free Trade Agreement (NAFTA), a 1994 accord between the United States, Canada, and Mexico. Though some jobs were lost through NAFTA, the agreement has generally led to increased trade, lower prices, and warm cooperation with our immediate neighbors.

Since then, however, globalization has barreled forward and led to the massive transfer of manufacturing and service jobs from the United States to Asia—especially China, Taiwan, India, and Korea. When the factories and service industries that anchored the economic base of thousands of communities in Pennsylvania, Ohio, Kentucky, and elsewhere disappeared, those communities collapsed. Unemployment shot up, families disintegrated, alcoholism and drug addiction increased, schools and parishes closed, crime rates climbed, and young people fled to urban areas. The pathetic scenes in Ohio described in JD Vance's *Hillbilly Elegy*[35] were multiplied in thousands of homes and villages throughout the Midwest and the South.

Late in Bill Clinton's second term, a *Time* magazine cover[36] featured a photo of Robert Rubin, Larry Summers, and Alan Greenspan as the

---

34 Friedman, Tom, "America, China and a Crisis of Trust," *The New York Times*, April 14, 2023.
35 Vance, J. D., *Hillbilly Elegy*, HarperCollins (2016).
36 *Time*, Feb. 15, 1999.

three supreme architects of Clinton's globalization policy, and the story gave it an unqualified endorsement. This was typical of the uncritical enthusiasm for globalization at the time. Donald Trump later demonstrated a genius for exploiting the grievances of millions of Americans, the sorts of people described in *Hillbilly Elegy*, and much of the unhappiness can be traced back to globalization.

Like most Americans, I believe in the value of competition and the advantages of open markets, but I think we have swept into globalization without sufficient consideration of the impact. As U.S. National Security Adviser Jake Sullivan stated in an April 2023 address at the Brookings Institution, "the prevailing assumption was that trade-enabled growth would be inclusive growth—that the gains of trade would end up getting broadly shared within nations." It turns out that the benefits have principally benefited the wealthy. Sullivan added, "The vision of public investment that had energized the American project in the postwar years—and indeed for much of our history—ha[s] faded. It ha[s] given way to a set of ideas that championed tax cutting and deregulation, privatization over public action, and trade liberalization as an end in itself."

Sullivan argued that trade policy needs to be more than tariff reduction. To rectify these errors, the Biden administration pursued a modern industrial and innovation strategy both at home and abroad, one that targeted sectors that are vital to economic growth and national security. The administration embraced the previously anathematized term "industrial policy" as essential to achieving "a foreign policy for the middle class."[37]

The Biden administration took a tempered and targeted approach to modifying globalization. Donald Trump, in his campaign for re-election in 2024, threatened a broad imposition of high tariffs, a policy that many economists worried could lead to inflation and higher costs for ordinary Americans and retaliatory tariffs on American goods. It's always hard to predict what will emerge in reality from Trump's rhetoric and bluster, but building a tariff wall around the United States presents a dangerous prospect.

---

37 Sullivan, Jake, "Renewing American Economic Leadership," April 27, 2023, speech released by the White House.

Since before World War II, America assumed a leadership role in the world, and since the war, the Atlantic alliance served as a powerful backup. As Roger Cohen of *The New York Times* wrote in 2023, "It is a mistake to underestimate the resiliency of democracies, buttressed by the transatlantic bond. Slow to anger, they are formidable in the breach."[38]

Alarmingly, America's reckless political polarization is having a profoundly unsettling impact on the country's foreign policy, signaling at home and abroad that the United States has grown unsure of its place in the world. Initially, the Biden administration enjoyed considerable success in putting together a broad coalition of countries supporting Ukraine as it resisted the Russian invasion led by President Vladimir Putin. Biden's robust response to Ukraine President Volodymyr Zelensky's request for help reassured NATO allies and partners who had expected an early victory by Russian forces. The Biden initiative was also in keeping with long-standing American values, supporting democracies and opposing blatant aggression. At first, the approach—working with allies, supplying money and equipment, not troops—found wide approval at home. Surveys showed that a strong consensus of Americans stood behind the administration. Most establishment Republican leaders, including Senate minority leader Mitch McConnell, backed Biden.

But Trump and a hard-core group of right-wing Republicans have pushed back against support to Ukraine, and, as this is written, it's not clear that American aid will continue to flow. There's a strong risk that the invasion by Putin—a notoriously bad actor in Russia and on the global stage—will succeed.

Meantime, during the 2024 campaign, Trump delivered a further shock to America's allies by claiming that as president he would invite Russia to "do whatever the hell they want" to NATO countries that were behind on their financial obligations to the treaty organization. GOP leaders compounded the trouble by downplaying the comment. America's traditional allies worry that during his second administration, Trump will withdraw the United States from NATO, until recently an unthinkable prospect.

The American role in the Hamas–Israel war has also raised serious questions about America's place in the world. After the vicious

---

[38] Cohen, Roger, *An Affirming Flame*, Alfred Knopf (2023), p. 44.

Hamas attack on Israel on October 7, 2023, President Biden was fulsome in his support for Israel. But Israeli Prime Minister Benjamin Netanyahu responded to the attack with a continuing, devastating offensive against Hamas in Gaza, killing thousands and obliterating great sections of the Palestinian territory. Much of the world and many Americans found the Israeli reaction far out of proportion, particularly given the harsh circumstances under which Gazans had been living for years. The Biden administration found itself unable to significantly restrain Netanyahu, ostensibly a close ally. And America's traditional support for Israel came under fire from a range of domestic critics, from left-leaning voters to right-wing Republicans. Nonetheless, Trump has indicated his full-throated support for Netanyahu, suggesting that the Israeli attacks in Gaza and against Hezbollah in Lebanon will not abate.

Both the Ukraine invasion and the Hamas–Israel war starkly illustrate how domestic politics is playing havoc with American global leadership. For the moment, those conflicts are largely obscuring an equally serious issue on the horizon: whether the U.S. should mount a major response to China if the Chinese government under Xi Jinping launches a military attack on Taiwan. Ukraine and Taiwan have some similarities. Over the centuries, Ukraine has been an integral part of Russia. Similarly, for thousands of years, the island of Taiwan was part of China.

At least until the latest political haggling, the leadership of both Republican and Democratic Parties reflected widespread support for continued robust backing of Taiwan, and opinion surveys show a similar attitude among the public.

But in a significant way, the Taiwanese situation is different from Ukraine's. As *New York Times* columnist Tom Friedman reported in April 2023, Chinese President Xi Jinping made it clear to Biden in their meeting in November 2022 that China is prepared to go to war to prevent the permanent independence of Taiwan.[39]

Among NATO members, the support for Taiwan is less than enthusiastic. While most oppose a military attempt by China to recover Taiwan, they would not support an American effort to prevent a takeover if the alternative were the risk of nuclear war. Virtually

---

39 Friedman, Tom, "America, China and a Crisis of Trust," *The New York Times*, April 14, 2023.

all European NATO members, in addition to Japan, have signaled their hesitancy; hence, there would be no Ukraine-style coalition. It's relevant that Russia, though nuclear-armed, is a regional power, declining in influence. China, also nuclear-armed, is a rising power vastly increasing its influence and in the view of many experts is on the way to replacing the United States as the world hegemon.

If it becomes certain that continued strong support for Taiwan could easily lead to military conflict between China and the United States, should the U.S. continue on the same course, risking nuclear war? My answer is the realist answer: no. Despite our sympathy for the Taiwanese and admiration for their achievement in establishing a viable democratic government, the fact remains that the island's separation was an accident flowing from the defeat in 1949 of the Nationalist forces by the Chinese Communist Party in the civil war that followed World War II. Nationalist forces led by President Chiang Kai-shek fled to Taiwan, and the Chiang-dominated authoritarian government eventually evolved into a vibrant democracy. Xi Jinping's determination to reunite Taiwan with mainland China enjoys widespread popular support in China.

The absorption of Taiwan by China would almost certainly follow the sad pattern of Hong Kong—increased political repression and replacement of democratic institutions through edicts emanating from the Communist Party–dominated government in Beijing. Still, acquiescing to that result is preferable to nuclear war. The outcome of such a war is almost unthinkable, but it would almost certainly lead to the death of millions of Americans and Chinese and utterly disrupt whatever order exists in the world.

In short, while encouraging a policy of restraint on both Beijing and Taipei and encouraging Beijing to have patience, the United States should prepare itself and its allies to see Taiwan reunited with mainland China, even if that's the result of a military takeover in Taiwan. Would such an outcome represent a serious setback for the United States' role in the world? Absolutely! Such is the inevitable outcome when a rising imperial power reduces the sway of a declining imperial power.

How would the Trump administration respond to a Chinese military takeover of Taiwan? Trump has made China a foil for his plans to raise tariffs, but at the same time he has cultivated a relationship with President Xi Jinping, a model of the type of autocratic leader Trump admires. He has occasionally talked tough on Taiwan. Nothing in his approach so far indicates that he has the savvy or foresight to manage the relationship between China and Taiwan to avoid a military crisis.

Overall, the election of Donald Trump to a second term in November 2024 throws the patterns of American postwar foreign policy into disarray, without in my view remotely improving the country's standing in the world. Based on his actions during his first term, his repeated comments, and his early appointments to his second administration, Trump's foreign policy comes into view as a muddle. It is somewhat isolationist and somewhat based on deal-making, largely financial, and it features an utterly un-American attraction to autocrats, such as Russia's Vladimir Putin, North Korea's Kim Jong Un, and Hungary's Viktor Orbán.

But Trump is also a wellspring of resentments, with a prowess for exploiting the resentments of others. And he is a champion of people who have stood by him (at least, until he tires of them). Both qualities course through his decision-making and could further degrade American policies, both foreign and domestic.

To borrow a euphemism, he doesn't play well with others around the globe. He has belittled longtime American allies and threatened the solidarity of NATO, one of the most effective defense alliances in world history. In the Pacific, the United States has recently formed an alliance with India and South Korea aimed at countering Chinese influence in the region; it's unclear whether that promising initiative will disappear under Trump.

His isolationist inclinations and affection for Putin go some way toward explaining his reluctance to give strong support to Ukraine's fight against the Russian incursion. At this writing, it's unclear how Trump's policy will develop, but his comments and those of his vice president, JD Vance, suggest that a Trump administration would pressure Ukraine to cede territory to Russia in return for a settlement of the war, effectively ratifying the Russian attack and accepting the norm that a big country can gobble a small one. Alarm bells would ring bracingly in other European nations—particularly the Baltic countries—and signal another blow to America's standing in the world.

A few paragraphs earlier, I described the United States as a "declining imperial power." I've reflected on the use of that language. Although I have long shared the view of financier and philanthropist Warren Buffett that "no one ever made money betting against the future of the United States," it is increasingly difficult to deny the accumulating evidence that U.S. authority and influence are waning, and the country is facing huge internal strains. While sharp political differences have been evident throughout American history, the current divisiveness in American society is unprecedented since the Civil War. Bipartisan cooperation is almost nonexistent. The fatal shootings of innocent Americans by lone gunmen now occur almost weekly, and still the carnage can't persuade Republican leaders to weaken their opposition to effective gun control. Despite firm evidence of a devastating climate threat to the planet, many political leaders—many, but not all of them Republican—fight effective environmental controls. Media institutions, such as those long-established television networks—ABC, NBC, and CBS—which for decades functioned as mediating filters for the public, have sunk in influence, replaced by noisy extremists on cable and the internet. Other institutions that long played a crucial role in creating and maintaining a stable society—churches, labor unions, public schools, and fraternal organizations—have atrophied and lost their sway.

The United States remains the wealthiest society in world history, but that wealth continues to be concentrated among the top 20% of Americans—and to a shocking degree, among the top 1%. Despite multiple Democratic regimes in Washington, the tax system remains heavily tilted toward upper-income Americans. Meantime, it is commonly acknowledged that the Internal Revenue Service is grossly underfunded and lacks the resources to scrutinize the returns of millionaires and billionaires who enjoy the services of accountants and lawyers to facilitate the circumvention of the law. Still, the Republican Party, which was divided over the prospect of Donald Trump's return to the presidency, remained united in its determination to starve the IRS of the staff resources required to police the tax returns of top payers. Some Republican leaders have a long history of fighting for balanced budgets. By adamantly refusing realistic funding for the IRS, they are ensuring that the massive budget deficits will continue.

I see little in Donald Trump's purported second-term agenda to suggest he cares about solving the problems confronting the country. He favors burning more fossil fuels (further raising climate concerns), wants to continue with lower taxes for the rich and corporations (aggravating the wealth divide between Americans), and enjoys making vulgar and cruel comments (continuing to debase our civic life). He seems to be filling his administration with mediocre and stained characters whose principal qualification is loyalty to him. In short, Trump hardly seems the figure to lead the country into a hopeful new era.

Still, the United States enjoys several notable strengths that a Trump administration could build on—if it doesn't clumsily undermine them. Thanks to President Barack Obama, most Americans now have access to reliable health care. Though public elementary and high schools in much of the country continue to decline (in large part due to the influence of teachers' unions), American higher education offers a bright spot. American universities dominate the top of the lists of best in the world. Equally important, access to elite American colleges and universities has expanded in recent years to an almost unbelievable degree. "Need-blind admission" policies have been adopted by most of the top schools, meaning that if a student qualifies academically, he or she can attend through some combination of scholarships and loans. The change will almost certainly have a positive impact on upward mobility in America at a time when upward mobility has otherwise slowed.[40] Affirmative action policies greatly expanded university access for thousands of African American, Latino, and Native American students. A recent Supreme Court ruling has knocked out affirmative action, but I expect schools will continue to find ways to advance minority admissions. The increased scrutiny of Ivy League institutions by congressional committees, sparked by accusations of antisemitism on campus following the outbreak of the Hamas–Israel conflict, may temporarily moderate this trend. But it is unlikely to completely reverse it.

---

40 Chetty, Raj, et al., "The Fading American Dream," *Science*, April 28, 2017.

The quality of American higher education has long been a magnet for students around the world, and it's had an overwhelmingly positive influence on other societies. The Fulbright program, financed by the U.S. government, has brought tens of thousands of students and professors to America's leading universities. Generously endowed American universities have financed the training of scientists and academic specialists in all fields who now populate the faculties of universities all over the world. Though the current conflict with China (not to speak of the proliferation of school shootings) may disrupt the flow of foreign students, the welcoming of those students should continue to spread American values.

There are other positive chords. The Information Revolution and the internet boom have been largely spurred by American ingenuity and business. Though the U.S. response to the COVID epidemic has been criticized, U.S. scientists were leaders in finding vaccines to fight the disease. The fact is that American science, business, and education still have the talent and resources to rally enormous efforts to accomplish astonishing things.

Sadly, I worry that much of that potential is threatened by the terrible disruption in our civic life. George Kennan's seminal containment theory dominated U.S. foreign policy in the decades after World War II and certainly played a key role in preserving the country's place as the center of world power. But in his famous "X" article in *Foreign Affairs* setting out his theory, he offered a significant stipulation that's often overlooked: The United States must "create among the peoples of the world generally the impression of a country which knows what it wants, which is coping successfully with the problems of its internal life and with the responsibilities of a World Power, and which has a spiritual vitality capable of holding its own among the major ideological currents of the time." Providence, Kennan added, has provided "the American people with this implacable challenge, has made their entire security as a nation dependent on their pulling themselves together and accepting the responsibilities of moral and political leadership that history plainly intended them to bear."[41]

Today, the United States does not offer its citizens or the rest of the world that moral and political leadership. The extreme polarization of American society, the erosion of influence of essential social

---

41 "The Sources of Soviet Conduct," p. 868.

institutions, the failure to protect citizens from repeated murders by deranged individuals, the gaps between the wealthy and the average citizen—all these factors and more indicate that America can no longer credibly assert that it remains a model to be emulated.

With the rise of China, the predominant influence that the United States wielded in world affairs over the last half century is not likely to continue. Still, the U.S. can retain its role as a powerful world leader. But it's not a matter of military might—the U.S. already has that, probably to excess. Rather, it will require restoring a consensus in American society to repair the damaged and neglected social fabric of the country; it will take re-establishing confidence in governmental institutions at all levels; above all, it will require making *e pluribus unum* a reality in America.

AUTHOR'S NOTE

When I look back on my nine decades of life, I recognize that one of my core values from an early age has been friendship. Many of my friendships grew out of my international work, and most enhanced it. But these weren't simply transactional relationships of passing convenience—they were genuine friendships in which we enjoyed each other's company and continued to see each other long after official business was concluded. In ways large and small, these friends have contributed immeasurably to this book.

My closest friendships began during my college years at St. John's. This included my two college roommates, Bill Kelsch and Bob Shafer, both of whom remained lifelong friends. Bill Kelsch was a tall man, six-foot-two, soft-spoken, and a gifted poet. He went on to become a lawyer in Mandan, North Dakota, where he had grown up and where his father had been the town lawyer. I would see Bill from time to time at St. John's reunions. Irene and I later welcomed him and Joan, his wife of 40 years, as guests in our apartment in Paris.

Bob Shafer and I co-founded an underground newspaper at St. John's that survived through only one edition. After he graduated from Georgetown Law School, Bob and I got together regularly in New York and Washington, where he headed the lobbying office of Pfizer. Bob was a sophisticated and handsome man with a sharp sense of humor. He did not get married until he was 40, and as he drew closer to that age he used to quip to his friends, "I either had to find a wife or a nurse." Winning Ellen to be his wife was a well-rewarded effort.

During my six years in Cambridge, both while studying and teaching in the government department at Harvard, I developed a number of friends with whom I would stay close for decades. I met many of them through the Harvard Catholic Club. This group included three law students and two graduate students. After we left Harvard, the six of us would meet regularly for lunch at the Harvard Club in New York City, gatherings that kept up on a fairly regular basis until 2015, when age, disability, and death intervened. The common ground of our bond was an interest in education and a common Catholic educational background.

The group included Dan O'Hearn, a brilliant Harvard Law student who clerked for U.S. Supreme Court Justice William Brennan and later served two decades on the New Jersey Supreme Court. Also in our group was George McCormick, a conservative Catholic from Brooklyn who later interrupted his busy New York law practice to serve a month each year in a poor African mission. The third law student was Frank Gallagher, who later led a small boutique law firm in his hometown of Doylestown, Pennsylvania. Our group also included Zdenek David, a Czech exchange student temporarily in the United States in 1946-47. When the Communist Party took over the Czech Republic, Zed was advised to remain in the United States. He received a scholarship to the history department at Harvard and eventually became the head librarian at the Woodrow Wilson Center for International Scholars in Washington, D.C. The second grad student was Jack Brennan, who came from Queens, New York, and spoke with the accent to go with it. He went on to become a professor of English history at Long Island University.

During my years on the Humphrey staff, I formed a close friendship with John Stewart, a savvy PhD from the University of Chicago who excelled as Humphrey's legislative assistant. He played an indispensable role in ensuring Humphrey's success in passing the Civil Rights Bill. Several years later, I gained an appreciation of Norman Sherman, Humphrey's press secretary, whose sharp sense of humor endeared him to the press. Ted Van Dyk, director of communications and a skilled and efficient editor, became an important ally on Vietnam, and in 1968 he became an influential traveling companion for the vice president. My closest friendship acquired during the Humphrey years was with Bob Hunter, a gifted writer and analyst who first surfaced during the vice presidential campaign in 1964. We later coedited a book, *Development Today: A New Look at U.S. Relations with the Poor Countries* (Praeger Publishing, 1972). Bob also consulted on the Public Opinion project and wrote the script for a documentary on that subject that won a local award. Bob would later serve on the National Security Council under President Carter. President Clinton appointed him as U.S. ambassador to NATO.

During my three decades at the Chicago Council, I developed close friendships with the directors of four other leading international NGOs in Europe and Japan, all of whom served at least 30 years in that position. This became an exclusive Thirty-Year Club. It included Karl Kaiser, director of the German Council on Foreign Relations; Thierry de Montbrial, director of the French Institute of International Relations; Cesare Merlini, director of the Italian Institute of International Affairs; and Tadashi Yamamoto, director of the Japan Center for International Exchange. We regularly shared program ideas, funding, and speaker contacts and participated in each other's conferences.

My long-term personal relationships had a broad reach. Often I made introductions or wrote recommendations for the friend or the friend's child. My closest Brazilian friend was Marcilio Marques Moreira, who would later become both the minister of finance of Brazil and the Brazilian ambassador to the United States. His daughter hoped to attend Georgetown University, and I called my friend Peter Krogh, dean of the School of Foreign Service at Georgetown, to recommend her. She ended up graduating with honors. Cultivated and low-key, Marcilio was well connected in the Brazilian establishment, and he became an important leader in the success of the Atlantic Conference.

My friendship with Joe Slater at the Ford Foundation introduced me to what I call the McCloy network, a tight circle of friends in Europe and the United States connected to John J. McCloy. McCloy had served as the U.S. High Commissioner in Germany from 1949 to 1953, and he later practiced law, became chairman of the board of the Ford Foundation, and advised presidents. In a celebrated article in *The New Yorker*, Richard Revere named McCloy the head of the American establishment.

Joe Slater served as deputy chief of staff to McCloy in Germany. A soft-spoken and courtly man with rare political antennae, Slater later became the deputy director of the International Division of the Ford Foundation and president of the Aspen Institute for Humanistic Studies. When Slater invited me to spend two weeks at the Aspen Institute in July 1974, I met an array of women and men who would become important figures in Germany. They included Marion Donhoff and Theo Sommer, who both served at various times as editor and publisher of *Die Zeit*, the leading weekly newspaper of Germany. Also among them were Richard von Weizsacker, who would go on to be president of Germany during its reunification; Kurt Biedenkopf, future prime minister of Saxony; and Karl Kaiser, longtime director of the German Council on Foreign Relations. All became important personal friends as well as important professional contacts. This is but one example of new friendships emanating from my friendship with Joe Slater. I would continue to see most of these friends regularly well into the 21st century. This was one of the most significant rewards of my half-century involvement in international affairs.

A curious postwar development in international affairs strongly broadened my network of friends and served to spread friendships generally between Americans and Europeans. In 1954, Prince Bernhard of the Netherlands launched what came to be known as the Bilderberg Conference, an annual meeting of leaders in and out of government in Europe and the U.S. to foster discussion of issues of concern and promote personal relationships. Originally funded by the Ford Foundation and the Carnegie Endowment for International Peace, the Bilderberg Conference became the prototype for U.S.-European conferences run by nonprofit institutes, including the Atlantic Conference and the North Atlantic Assembly. Conferences of that sort didn't occur in earlier periods of American history, and they didn't appear elsewhere in the world until later, when the Trilateral Commission, which followed a similar pattern, brought in Japan. The conferences warmed relations between countries, and many participants became close personal friends, a feature of the meetings I particularly enjoyed. Two of my most valued friendships formed at the Chicago Council on Foreign Relations were with John

F. Manley and Shirley Welsh Ryan. Both were longtime Council board members, generous financial supporters and outstanding civic and humanitarian leaders.

The cultivation of these friendships took time, thought, and sensitivity to the interests and priorities of others, while I sometimes had to set aside my own self-interest. The relationships might have grown from work, but they were based on shared interests, shared values, shared purposes, and in many cases, a common culture. In scrutinizing my records running up to the year 2022, I counted 75 individuals whom I considered friends, sharply distinguished from acquaintances. Some of these people of course are now dead. And at age 92, I know that my network of current friends will keep diminishing. But maintaining these friendships has brought great personal joy to me. Given the troubled state of the country as I write this, I would like to see a reawakening awareness of the joy and benefits of building friendships. I think that would redound to the advantage of all of us.

ACKNOWLEDGMENTS

Many people have assisted me in the preparation of this book. My deep appreciation goes to Roger Cohen for his generous and insightful introduction; also to Richard Babcock for his work editing the text; to Ambassador Robert Hunter for his review of the manuscript; and to close friends Marlise Simons and Alan Riding for their advice and counsel.

I would like to thank my children, Mary Ellen Rielly, Catherine Rielly, Tom Rielly, and John Rielly, for agreeing to lengthy interviews and for their many years of encouragement, support, and love; and my siblings Mary Murray, James Rielly, and Bernard Rielly for similar interviews and close friendship over many decades.

In addition to indispensable help in researching and editing the book, my wife, Irene, has never stopped loving and believing in me. Each day we share brings renewed joy.

INDEX

Note: Page references followed by *i* refer to photos.

A

Acheson, Dean, 21, 166
Adlai Stevenson Institute of International Affairs, 129-133
Afghanistan conflict, 168
Allende, Salvador, 42-43, 44, 45-46
Alliance for Progress
    author joins State to work on, 26-28
    ending, 2, 6, 40-41
    European support for, 33
    Humphrey's support for, 6-7, 28-29, 31-32, 39-41
    Kennedy's goals for, 2, 5, 26-27, 166
    political opposition to, 2, 28, 39-40
America First view, 1
Americans for Democratic Action, 93
Anderson, Mary, 161
Anderson, Paul, 161
Andreas, Dwayne, 116, 144
anti-communism, 16-17, 42-47, 59.
    See also communism
anti-war protesters, 92-93
Apple, Johnny, 94, 122
Arbatov, Georgi, 148
Arms Control and Disarmament Agency, 34
arms control, Humphrey's interest, 34-35
Asia fact-finding mission (1966), 72-84
Atlantic Community Development Group for Latin America, 33
Atlantic Conferences, 142-143, 156, 184

B

Bader, Bill, 132
Baker, James, 157
Ball, George, 62, 69, 121
Barnett, Doak, 112
Bassetti, Carla, 161
Bassetti, Piero, 161
Bay of Pigs incident, 165, 171
Beer, Samuel, 18, 26
Bell, Dave, 127, 146
Bennett, Douglas, 35
Benton, William, 65-66, 125
Bhutto, Zulfikar Ali, 79
Biden, Joe, 143, 150-151, 168, 173
Biedenkopf, Kurt, 185
Bilderberg Conference, 185
Blair, Bill, 83
Boggs, Hale, 117
Bohlen, Charles, 166
Bolling, Landrum, 132, 146
bombing of North Vietnam
    advisors favoring, 58, 60
    Humphrey speeches favoring, 92
    Humphrey's opposition, 60-61, 110, 113-115, 117-118, 120-122
    Johnson's announced halt, 124
    Johnson's reductions, 95
    Thai support, 77, 78
Bosnian Civil War, 168
Bouton, Marshall, 24, 156, 157
Bowles, Chester, 35
Brandon, Henry, 90
Brandt, Willy, 70, 101*i*, 144
Brennan, Jack, 183
Broder, David, 147
Bryan, John, 105*i*, 156
Brzezinski, Zbigniew, 92, 112-113, 115-116, 152
Bui Diem, 123
Bundy, Bill, 58

Bundy, McGeorge
- author as replacement instructor for, 23-24
- in early Vietnam policy discussions, 58, 61-62
- as head of Ford Foundation, 126-127, 131-132, 146
- participation in Asia fact-finding mission, 73
- personal qualities, 65
- response to Pleiku attack, 60

Bureau of Intelligence and Research (INR), 88
Bush, Barbara, 154
Bush, George H. W., 103i, 145, 154, 168
Bush, George W., 168
Byrnes, John, 131-132

C

Califano, Joseph, 66
Calloway, John, 101i
Camp David Accords, 167
Carnegie Endowment for International Peace, 141-142, 152
Carter, Jimmy, 150, 167
Catholicism, 11, 19, 22, 23
Cavalier, ND, years, 10-12
Central Intelligence Agency (CIA)
- author's positive impressions of, 17
- Chilean election efforts, 43, 44-46
- Church Committee revelations, 17
- Ford Foundation work with, 127-128
- NSA support, 15-16
- post-World War II covert actions, 43-44

charter flights, Council funding from, 138, 140, 141
Chennault, Anna, 123
Chicago Committee, 140
Chicago Community Trust, 153
Chicago Council on Foreign Relations
- Atlantic Conferences, 142-143, 156, 184
- author's candidacy for executive director, 134, 135, 138-139
- author's initial goals for, 140-141
- financial support, 138, 153-154, 156
- history, 135-138
- noteworthy world leaders invited during author's tenure, 143-146
- progress under author's leadership, 154-157
- public opinion survey on U.S. foreign policy, 146-148
- support for *Foreign Policy* journal, 151-152

Chicago Tribune, 137-138, 155-156, 157
Chilean presidential elections, 42-46
China's threat to Taiwan, 175-177
Chirac, Jacques, 144
Church, Frank, 53, 85, 142
Church Committee, 17, 44, 46
church-state relations, 19-20, 22-23, 36
Clemenceau, Georges, 135-136
Clifford, Clark, 94
climate change, 178
Clinton, Bill, 168, 172-173
Clinton, Hillary, 155
Cogley, John, 23
Cole, William, 134, 135
Colombia, 28
Commission, Kerner, 117
communism
- author's opposition, 17
- containment policy, 166-167, 180
- domino theory fears, 46, 48, 50
- fears of takeover in Chile, 42-46
- Reagan's opposition, 145

Congress for Cultural Freedom, 128

Connell, Bill
  author's initial interview with, 31
  dislike for author, 36, 54
  participation in Asia fact-finding mission, 74
  support for Humphrey's presidential campaign, 96
containment policy, 166–167, 180
Cooper, Richard, 152
Cordes, Robert, 156
corporate service program of Chicago Council, 141
Coulter, Tom, 138
Cram, Cleveland, 18, 37
Cram, Mary, 37
Cresson, Edith, 100i
Cuban missile crisis, 31, 165
Cyr, Arthur, 153, 154, 156

D

Daley, Richard J., 144
Daley, Richard M., 144–145
Danforth Fellowship, 18, 21
David, Zdenek, 183
de Gaulle, Charles, 50
Democratic National Convention (1968), 116–119
Dentzer, William, 27
DeSantis, Ron, 151
Deutsch, Karl, 24
Development Today (Hunter and Rielly, eds.), 184
domino theory, 3, 46, 48, 50–51
Donhoff, Marion, 185
Dorado Beach conference, 142–143
Dudman, Dick, 90
Dukakis, Michael, 145
Dulles, Allen, 17, 43
Duran, Julio, 43

E

education, importance to Rielly family, 10
Eger, Edmond, 138
Eisenhower, Dwight, 49
Elliott, William Y., 19
Ellsberg, Daniel, 76
Encuentro Siglo Veinto program, 142
Erhard, Ludwig, 70
Erlander, Tage, 70

F

Fitzgerald, Des, 45
FitzGerald, Frances, 45
Foley, Eugene, 91
Food for Peace program, 35
Ford, Gerald, 146, 147
Ford Foundation
  author's employment after Humphrey election loss, 126–133
  author's job offers from, 68–69
  funding for Chicago Council programs, 141–142, 153
  public opinion survey funding, 146
  work with CIA, 127–128
Foreign Affairs journal
  article on AFP, 6, 41
  importance of, 151–152
  "X" article, 166, 180
foreign policy. *See also* Chicago Council on Foreign Relations; Vietnam policy
  author's academic move to, 23–24
  author's observations on current trends, 171–181
  domino theory influence, 48–49, 50
  for Humphrey's presidential campaign, 112–115, 117–118
  Humphrey's role as VP, 55, 66, 69–71
  leadership's influence, 169–171
  post-World War II trends, 48–49, 149, 150, 165–169
  public opinion survey, 146–148

public's role debated, 148–151
Truman Doctrine impact, 48, 167
University Club speech, 157
Foreign Policy journal, 151–152
foundations, efforts to tax, 131–132
Fraleigh, Albert, 58–60
Franco, Francisco, 166
Frankel, Max, 89
Freeman, Orville, 66, 74, 113
Frei, Eduardo, 43, 44–45
Friedrich Ebert Foundation, 32–33
Fulbright, William, 54, 85, 87
Fulbright Scholarship, 19–20

G

Galbraith, John Kenneth, 80, 93
Gallagher, Frank, 183
Gandhi, Indira, 80
Gardner, Richard, 63
Gaza war, 174–175
Gelb, Leslie, 24
George Polk Awards, 129
Germany
    archbishop's delegation from, 69
    author's visits, 154–155
    chancellor candidates' meetings with president, 70
    Chicago Council support from, 143, 153
    fascism's rise in 1930s, 136
    McCloy's service in, 184–185
    political parties' foundations, 32–33
Geyelin, Phil, 85
Ginsburg, David, 117
globalization, 172–173
Goldwater, Barry, 50, 54–55
Goodwin, Richard, 117
Gorbachev, Mikhail, 104i, 144, 145, 150, 167
Gorbachev, Raisa, 144, 154
Grant, James, 134
Gray, Jack, 147, 156
Greeley, Andrew, 20–21
Greenspan, Alan, 172–173

Gremillion, Joseph, 39
Gulf of Tonkin resolution, 53–54
gun control, 178

H

Habib, Phil, 75–76
Halberstam, David, 130, 153
Hale, William, 135
Hamas-Israel war, 174–175
Hand, Lloyd, 74
Harriman, Averill
    counsel against continuing war, 95
    criticism of anti-war arguments, 87
    as foreign policy leader, 166
    participation in Asia fact-finding mission, 73, 76–77, 80, 81, 82, 98i
Harris, Chauncey, 132
Harris, Fred, 113
Harvard University, author's years at, 18–24
Hellinger, James, 163
Hellinger, Jason, 108i, 163
Hellinger, Riley, 108i, 163
Hersh, Seymour, 116
Hibbard, Susan Follansbee, 135
higher education in America, 179–180
Ho Chi Minh, 48–49
Hoge, James, 101i, 140–141
Holbrooke, Richard, 152
Holt, Harold, 81–82
Hong Kong, 176
Hughes, Tom
    author's friendship with, 57, 88–89
    as Carnegie Endowment president, 152
    decision to stay at State Department, 69
    departure from Humphrey's staff, 35–36
    opposition to Vietnam escalation, 50, 63–65, 66
Humphrey, Hubert
    Alliance for Progress support, 6–7, 28–29, 31–32, 39–41
    Asia fact-finding mission (1966), 72–84, 98i

Asia mission aftermath, 84–87
Asia trip in 1967, 94
attempted Vietnam policy change as presidential candidate, 112–115, 117–118
author joins staff, 31
author's advice to on Vietnam escalation, 50–52
criticized for Latin American labor group comments, 69–70
deterioration of relationship with LBJ, 65–68, 110
early discussions on Vietnam policy as vice president, 59–62
emergence as likely Democratic nominee in 1968, 109–112
first speech on Vietnam, 53
Hughes memo incident, 63–65, 66
influence on author, 170
intervention for visiting European leaders, 70–71
as leading vice presidential candidate in 1964, 6, 53
nomination in 1968, 116–119
Pacem in Terris speech, 62–66
personal qualities, 31, 109–110, 170
pictured with author's children, 99i
political rise, 30–31, 34
presidential campaign, 120–125
switch to support for Vietnam War, 85–87
as vice presidential candidate in 1964, 54–55
as Vietnam War booster, 92–94
Hunter, Bob, 184
Huntington, Sam, 112–113, 142, 151–152
Hutcherson, John, 161
Hutchins, Robert Maynard, 62–63
Hynes, Sister M. Celine, 99i, 100i, 159, 160

I

Internal Revenue Service, 178
International Association for Cultural Freedom, 128–129
Iraq conflict, 168
isolationism
  championed by McCormick in *Tribune*, 137
  Chicago Council founded in response to, 135–136
  renewed concerns after Nixon resignation, 146
  twentieth century trends in U.S., 24, 149
Israel-Hamas war, 174–175

J

Javits, Jacob, 33
John D. and Catherine T. MacArthur Foundation, 153
Johnson, Lyndon Baines
  administration debates on Vietnam policy in 1965, 57–62
  announcement of decision not to run in 1968, 95
  aversion to information leaks, 53, 62, 66, 90
  deterioration of Humphrey's relationship with, 65–68, 110
  early Vietnam policy, 49
  lukewarm support for Humphrey in 1968, 120, 122, 124
  Nixon favored by, 120
  opposition to Humphrey's campaign policy on Vietnam, 114–115, 117–118, 120, 122
  orders for Humphrey's 1966 Asia trip, 72–73
  responsibility for Vietnam War, 171
  succession to presidency, 39
  Vietnam discussions after election win, 57–58

K

Kaiser, Karl, 104i, 184, 185
Kelsch, Bill, 182
Kelsch, Joan, 182
Kennan, George F., 149-150, 166, 180
Kennedy, Edward "Teddy," 112
Kennedy, John F.
    Alliance for Progress goals, 2, 5, 26-27, 166
    assassination, 38-39
    church-state relations issue in presidential campaign, 22-23
    commitment of advisors to Vietnam, 49
    Eugene McCarthy's relationship with, 37-38
    foreign policy, 165-166
    Humphrey's relationship with, 34
    influence on author, 170-171
    personal qualities, 170-171
Kennedy, Robert "Bobby," 82-83, 93, 95, 111-112
Kerensky, Alexander, 136
Kerstein, Hanneke, 161
Kerstein, Tom, 161
Keynes, John Maynard, 136
KGB agents, 91
Kirkpatrick, Clayton, 155-156
Kissinger, Henry
    alliance with Nixon campaign, 115-116, 122-123
    with author's children at Chicago Council gathering, 100i
    domino theory concerns, 46
    as Harvard instructor, 19
    role in Nixon's foreign policy, 167
Kittikachorn, Thanom, 77
Kohl, Hannelore, 143, 154, 155
Kohl, Helmut
    appearances for Chicago Council, 106i, 143
    author's friendship with, 143, 154-155
    democratic principles, 2
    participation in first Atlantic Conference, 142-143
    support for Chicago Council, 143, 153
Kohl-Richter, Maike, 155
Konrad Adenauer Foundation, 32
Korean conflict, 137
Kosygin, Alexei, 61
Kraft, Joseph, 50
Krogh, Peter, 184
Ky, Nguyen Cao, 72, 74-75, 94

L

Laise, Carol, 74
Lansdale, Edward, 50, 58-60, 76
Laos, 77-78
Laski, Harold, 20
Latin America
    Alliance for Progress goals for, 26-27, 41-42
    Chilean election meddling, 42-46
    support of labor unions in, 69-70
Legion d'Honneur, 100i
LeMay, Curtis, 50, 111
Lewis, Anthony, 22
liberal internationalism, 1, 8, 166
liberalism at St. John's, 14-15
Lilly Endowment, 132
Lippmann, Walter, 50, 89, 149-150, 151
Lisagor, Peter, 90
Lodge, Henry Cabot, 75
Logevall, Fredrik, 64
London School of Economics and Political Science, 20
Louis Harris and Associates, 146-147
Lovett, Robert, 166
Lowenstein, Allard, 16, 93

M

MacArthur Foundation, 153
Manley, John, 156, 185-186
Mann, Thomas, 40, 41
Mansfield, Mike, 34, 85
Manshel, Warren, 151-152
Marcos, Ferdinand, 83
Marques Moreira, Marcilio, 184
Marshall Plan, 26
Martin, Graham, 78-79
McCarthy, Eugene
    considered for vice presidency, 54
    Humphrey's relationship with, 37, 38
    presidential campaign, 95, 111-112
    refusal to endorse Humphrey, 121, 125
    as St. John's graduate, 15
McCloskey, Robert, 18, 23
McCloy, John, 166, 184-185
McCormick, Colonel Robert, 137
McCormick, George, 183
McCormick Foundation, 156
McGovern, George, 60, 112
McNally, Tom, 161
McNamara, Robert, 45, 51-52, 58, 171
McNeill, William H., 132
Meany, George, 69-70
Menzies, Robert, 80
Merlini, Cesare, 104i, 184
Midgley, Elizabeth, 89
Mills, Wilbur, 131
Mitchell, John, 123
Mondale, Walter, 113, 142
Montbrial, Thierry de, 104i, 184
Morgenthau, Hans, 50
Moyers, Bill, 65
Murray, John Courtney, 19, 22
Muskie, Edmund, 118

N

National Federation of Catholic College Students, 15, 16
National Security Council, 60-61, 62
National Student Association, 15-16, 27
Nelson, Bryce, 53, 55
Netanyahu, Benjamin, 175
Neto, Delfin, 142
New York Council on Foreign Relations, 139, 151-152
Ngo Dinh Diem, 49
Nixon, Richard
    anti-communist efforts in Latin America, 45-46
    attention to public opinion, 150
    efforts to stall Paris peace talks in 1968, 122-124
    nomination in 1968, 111, 115
    realist foreign policy, 167
No More Vietnams? (Pfeffer, ed.), 130
Noble, Fiona Elizabeth Rielly, 105i, 163
North American Free Trade Agreement, 172
North Atlantic Treaty Organization (NATO), 48, 71, 149, 168, 174, 175-176
North Vietnam bombings. See bombing of North Vietnam
Northwestern University teaching job, 162

O

Oakeshott, Michael, 20
Obama, Barack, 168
O'Brien, Larry, 120
O'Hearn, Dan, 183
oil crisis, 147
oil policy, 171
Ordaz, Gustavo Diaz, 95, 96
Organization of American States, 32
Ossa, Sergio, 38-39, 44
Overseas Development Council, 134-135

P

Pacem in Terris conference, 62–66
Pahlavi Center, 130
Paris peace talks, 110, 115, 116, 122–124
peace plank, 117–118
Pembina County Fair, 11, 97i
Pinochet, Augusto, 46, 167
PlanetOut, 163
Pleiku attack, 60
Polk, George, 129
Polk, William, 129–133
Pons, Henrietta, 160–161
Potter, Phil, 79
The Price of Power (Hersh), 116
public opinion survey on U.S. foreign policy, 146–148
Putin, Vladimir, 174
Pye, Lucian, 113

R

Rauh, Joe, 93
Read, Ben, 57, 61, 73
Reagan, Nancy, 154
Reagan, Ronald, 145, 150, 167
realism, 8, 166, 167
Reischauer, Edwin, 113–114
Relly, Gavin, 105i
research program of Chicago Council, 141
Reston, James, 114
Richter, Maike, 155
Rielly, Bernard, 102i, 164
Rielly, Catherine, 21, 100i, 102i, 158, 159, 161, 163
Rielly, Elizabeth (Downs)
    courtship and marriage, 20–21
    disappointment at Humphrey's loss, 126
    separation and divorce, 158–159, 160
    Virgin Islands trip, 56
Rielly, Irene (Diedrich), 102i, 103i, 155, 161–162

Rielly, Jim, 102i, 163–164
Rielly, John E.
    activities in retirement, 162–164
    approached by foreign agents, 91
    arguments against Vietnam escalation, 50–52
    Asia mission report and aftermath, 84–87
    Asia trip in 1967, 94
    assessment of Humphrey senatorial staff, 35–36
    attempts to revive Alliance for Progress, 6–7
    Bill Connell's antipathy toward, 36, 54
    Chicago Council's progress under, 154–157
    childhood and family life, 9–13
    continued inquiries about Vietnam War status, 88–90
    Dorado Beach conference, 142–143
    early work on Humphrey's staff, 31–32, 34–35
    end of first marriage, 158–159
    enduring friendships, 182–186
    as executive director candidate for Chicago Council on Foreign Relations, 134, 135
    Ford Foundation work, 126–133
    Harvard graduate studies, 18–23
    Helmut Kohl's friendship with, 143, 154–155
    home life as vice presidential staff member, 72
    initial goals for Chicago Council, 140–141
    joins Humphrey staff, 29, 31
    at Mexico City gathering in 1968, 94–96
    most influential leaders for, 170–171
    noteworthy world leaders invited to Chicago by, 143–146
    observations on current trends in foreign policy, 171–181

Overseas Development Council job, 134–135
participation in Asia fact-finding mission, 72–84, 98i
photo gallery, 97–108
post-divorce family life and second marriage, 159–162
reflections on decision to stay with vice president's staff, 68–69
retirement from Chicago Council, 157
Roger Cohen's tribute to, 1–4
State Department work, 26–29
teaching at Harvard, 23–25, 165
undergraduate years at St. John's, 14–18
Vietnam Task Force work, 113
Rielly, John (son), 56, 100i, 102i, 158, 159, 161, 163
Rielly, Mary, 102i
Rielly, Mary Ellen, 21, 100i, 102i, 158, 159, 161, 162–163
Rielly, Mary (sister), 102i, 163
Rielly, Tom, 56, 100i, 102i, 158, 159, 161, 163
Roberts, Chalmers, 90
Robertson, George, 157
Rockefeller, David, 116, 126
Rolling Thunder, 61, 110. *See also* bombing of North Vietnam
Roosevelt, Franklin D., 12–13, 149
Rosenfeld, Stephen S., 147
Ross, Lotti, 156
Rubin, Robert, 172–173
Rusk, Dean, 58, 63, 91
Russell, Richard, 84
Russian invasion of Ukraine, 168, 174, 177
Ryan, Shirley Welsh, 105i, 156, 185–186

S

Saito, Hiroshi, 136
Salazar, Antonio, 21, 166
Salinger, Pierre, 117
Saudi Arabia, 147
Schlesinger, Arthur, 18–19, 26, 93

Seith, Alex, 135, 138–139
Senate (U.S.), Humphrey's status in, 33–34
September 11 attacks, 168
Sevareid, Eric, 85
Shafer, Bob, 15, 16, 182
Shafer, Ellen, 182
Sherman, Norman, 35, 74, 79, 122, 183
Shields, Jeff, 107i, 156
Shulman, Marshall, 92, 112
Shultz, George, 167
Simmons, Adele, 153
Slater, Joseph, 68, 112, 184–185
Smith, Bromley, 61
Smith, Hermon "Dutch," 139
Sommer, Theo, 185
Sorensen, Ted, 117
Souvanna Phouma, 77–78
Soviet Union
  author approached by agents of, 91
  Brzezinski's expertise on, 92
  concerns about Vietnam involvement, 52, 60, 61
  Humphrey's approach to dealing with, 31, 35
  NATO founded in response to, 48
  support for Allende candidacy, 43
  support for international organizations, 15–16, 127–128
  support for revolutionary groups, 43–44
  suppression of Czech liberalization, 117
Springsteen, George, 62
Squawk newspaper, 17–18
Squirru, Rafael, 32
St. James Academy, 12, 13
St. John's University, 14–18
Stanford University protesters, 92–93
State Department (U.S.), 26–29, 57
Stephan, Edmund, 156
Stevenson, Adlai II, 55, 129, 136
Stevenson, Adlai III, 135, 139
Stewart, John, 35, 183

Stone, Shepard, 127, 128
Sullivan, Jake, 173
Summers, Larry, 172-173
Symonds, Judith, 161
Szulc, Tad, 55, 89, 90-91

T

Taft, Robert, 149
Tagge, George, 139
Taiwan, 3-4, 175-177
tariffs, 173
teaching jobs in retirement, 162
Tet Offensive, 94-95
Thai communique, 78-79, 85
Thailand stops on Asia mission, 77, 78
Thatcher, Margaret, 106i, 144, 156
Thieu, Nguyen Van, 74-75, 94
Thomson, Jim
    campaign role in 1964, 55
    departure from Johnson administration, 69
    early input on Vietnam policy, 50, 53
    participation in Asia fact-finding mission, 74, 76, 81
Thurmond, Strom, 28, 32, 84
trade barriers, 172-173
Trilateral Commission, 145, 185
Truman, Harry, 48, 63, 149
Truman Doctrine, 48, 167
Trump, Donald, 151, 173, 174, 175, 176-177, 179

U

Ukraine invasion, 168, 174, 177
universities in America, 179-180
University Club speech, 157
University of California, San Diego, 162
University of Chicago, 129-133
Utley, Clifton, 136, 137

V

Valencia, Guillermo Leon, 28
Valenti, Jack, 74, 77, 80, 83
Van Dyk, Ted, 35, 84, 113, 114, 115, 147, 183
Vance, JD, 169
Videla, Guillermo, 44
Viet Cong, 49, 52, 60, 82-83
Vietnam policy
    administration debates in 1965, 57-62
    Democratic plank in 1968, 116-118
    Hughes's memo opposing escalation, 63-65
    Humphrey's attempt to change for 1968 campaign, 112-115, 117-118
    under JFK, 171
Vietnam Task Force, 112-113
Vietnam War
    author's arguments against, 3, 50-52
    beginning of U.S. combat role, 68
    as dominant campaign issue, 110-111
    events leading up to, 48-53
    growing domestic opposition, 93, 95
    Humphrey's change of view toward, 85-87, 92-93
    Humphrey's early opposition to, 59-65, 66
    negotiations to end, 110, 115, 116, 122-124

W

Wallace, George, 111
war on terror, 168
wealth concentration, 178
Webb, Jack, 15
Weinberger, Caspar, 145
Weizsacker, Richard von, 185
Westmoreland, William, 75
White, Theodore H., 124
Wicker, Tom, 77, 79, 82
Williams, Violet, 74
Wise Men, 7-8, 166
Wright, Louise Leonard, 139

X
"X" article, 166, 180
Xi Jinping, 175, 176, 177

Y
Yamamoto, Tadashi, 184
Yeltsin, Boris, 154

Z
Zelensky, Volodymyr, 174

Printed in the United States
by Baker & Taylor Publisher Services